BOOKMARK
NOW

BOOKMARK
NOW

Writing in Unreaderly Times

• • • • • • • • • • • • •

Edited by KEVIN SMOKLER

BASIC
BOOKS

A Member of the Perseus Books Group
New York

Published by Basic Books
A Member of the Perseus Books Group

Basic Books are available at special discounts for bulk purchases
in the United States by corporations, institutions, and other
organizations. For more information, please contact the Special
Markets Department at the Perseus Books Group, 11 Cambridge
Center, Cambridge MA 02142; or call (617) 252-5298 or
(800) 255-1514; or e-mail special.markets@perseusbooks.com.

Designed by Trish Wilkinson
Set in 11-point Goudy by the Perseus Books Group

Library of Congress Cataloging-in-Publication Data

Bookmark now : writing in unreaderly times / edited by
Kevin Smokler.
    p.   cm.
  ISBN 0-465-07844-3 (pbk. : alk. paper)
  1. Authorship. 2. Books and reading. 3. Authors and
readers. I. Smokler, Kevin.
PN137.B66 2005
808'.02—dc22   2005003358

05   06   07   /   10   9   8   7   6   5   4   3   2   1

For my Uncle Barry,
who I know writes alongside me.

CONTENTS

THE NOW

THE FUTURE

INTRODUCTION:
THE FUTURE IS NOW

In June 2004, the National Endowment for the Arts warned every book lover in America that the sky was falling. Publishing a report entitled *Reading at Risk,* the NEA concluded, from twenty years of data and a sampling of nearly seventeen thousand subjects, that "literary reading" (defined as anything fictional, including novels, plays, short stories, and poetry) had dropped sharply across every age, ethnic, economic, and geographic group in the nation. "America can no longer take active and engaged literacy for granted," declared NEA chairman Dana Gioia. If nothing changed, he warned, a well-read citizenry would be a thing of the past, a "vast cultural impoverishment" the result. Although Chairman Gioia stressed that the crisis had "no single solution and no single cause," the report didn't waste any time noting that as rates of reading slid, consumption of television, video games, and online media were swelling menacingly like a tumor on America's cultural consciousness.

All month long the report winged its way across newspapers, public radio airwaves, online discussion boards, and literary weblogs. Judgments were swift. Nobody brought up *Reading at Risk* and then said, "I need more data before I can tell you what I think." If you loved books, you either (a) were shocked, or (b) figured the NEA was simply saying what you had known all along. Given a minute, you probably said, (a) "Something has to be done," or (b) "Nothing can be done." Example A: Mitch Kaplan, owner of Miami's Books and Books, one of the country's most successful independents, called the report "our call to arms." Example B: In an imperious op-ed in the *New York Times*, writer Andrew Solomon bellowed that "a crisis in reading is a crisis in national health. . . . A crisis in reading is a crisis in national politics," then proposed no solution. No, wait; he did: "To encourage that great thrill of finding kinship in shared experiences of books." Like no one had thought of that yet.

I took a lot of calls and e-mails about the report that month and tried to stay true to my initial reaction. It made me sad. But something beneath that disappointment stunk up the joint, double-talk that proclaimed us to be living in a new kind of nightmare for American literacy while blaming the same old bogeymen. If online reading was eating away at book reading, how did we explain literary weblogs that commanded thousands of readers a day, or book recommendations and dialogue as crucial features in the next generations of social software? If young people were reading less than any other demographic group, how did we dismiss the revolution in young adult literature brought on by J. K. Rowling and Lemony Snicket, or the best-selling careers of twenty-something favorites like David Sedaris, Nick Hornby, Zadie Smith, and Jonathan Safran Foer?

I didn't quibble with *Reading at Risk*'s findings or methodology, since I'm not a statistician and the "what" of the report seemed more salient than the "how." But I didn't at all like the collective reaction from the media that viewed the report as a national emergency and the solution as a tsktsk. Were we simply a country of morons fulfilling our insipid destiny? Could we blame sexier, flashier media options with which the humble book couldn't compete? Those are pat, elitist answers to a complex problem, and America's reading public, however big or small, deserves better. If many factors are to blame, as Chairman Gioia asserted, surely some come from inside, from the industries and institutions that depend on a healthy reading populace for their very survival and yet seem to be losing more of it every generation.

For starters, it's no help that being well read has an enormous image problem in this country, and those who claim to be most bibliophilic are as much accomplice as advocate. We authors give dull, mumbly readings at bookstores and see interaction with readers, at best, as tedious distraction and, at worst, a frighteningly awkward social predicament. Universities, local lecture series, and writers' conferences are enablers, presenting writers in hushed, reverent tones, as if they were dangerous animals on safari. When books do show up on television, they are seen as playthings of the affluent (*Gilmore Girls*), the urbane (*Will and Grace*), or the middle-aged clad in tweed (*CSPAN's Book TV*). And when was the last time you heard public radio, that vanguard of a well-read America, treat an author like a human being, warts and all, instead of with the quiet deference reserved for an elderly relative at Thanksgiving?

Is it any wonder that the average person, who might consume movies, television, and music with gusto, ignores literature? That they see books as all good and well for the Lexus and latte set but not sexy enough for Saturday night and not real enough for the world of jobs, rent, and fun when you can manage it?

We lusty bibliophiles know that reading, unlike just about anything else, is both good for you *and* loads of fun. But look at how literature presents itself in public; then say loudly, "Where the hell is the fun?"

I may have missed it, but not once during the cacophony surrounding *Reading at Risk* did I see a representative from the publishing industry stand up and take some responsibility. On the one hand, who could blame the publishers' representatives? It's not a great business strategy when your market is evaporating to say that you brought it upon yourself. On the other, dire conditions are often the best catalyst for radical, revolutionary ideas. You'd think at least one publisher would seize the opportunity and say that yes, despite all this bad news, we will take the wheel, turn this ghost ship around, and make tomorrow better than today for books.

No one did.

• • •

I turned thirty-one this year, and working with books is the only adult job I've been able to keep. In just under four years of reviewing, analyzing, and creating online communities around contemporary literature, I've seen Oprah spar with Jonathan Franzen and Dave Eggers turn traditional publishing on its head. I've seen *This American Life* do for books what *The Daily Show* has done for politics, spoken word poets appear on HBO alongside the women of *Sex and the City*, and authors in their sixties and seventies get turned on to blogging. I've seen George Plimpton, Gwendolyn Brooks, and Joseph Heller pass on and Zoe, the eight-year-old who consistently wins my local poetry slam, come into her own.

This is an amazing time for books. If reading and literature are in crisis, it certainly isn't one of apathy but one of seismic rumblings of change that will have a profound effect on the future. The world of books will be totally different tomorrow than it is today, and it will happen much sooner than we think. And since I've never been on time for any trend in my life—not indie rock, breakdancing, or parachute pants—I'd rather be at the party now than in an imagined past when a nation read together, authors walked as gods on earth, and publishers went home fat and happy every afternoon.

The writers in this book weren't around for this age of literature, if it ever really existed (and I don't think it did). The oldest are in their early forties, the youngest nineteen. They are the second generation to be raised by television, the first to grow up with video games in childhood and the Internet in college. They've chosen literary lives not only when the arts offer more lucrative options (club DJ, independent filmmaker, hip-hop mogul) and are doing so when more stimuli and information compete for an audience's attention than at any time in history. It's worth asking why they bother. Even more it's worth learning about the state and future of literature from their choices.

A generation ago, young writers could not begin or accelerate their careers by publishing online as essayists Pamela Ribon,

Elizabeth Spiers, Neal Pollack, and Douglas Rushkoff have done. They rarely had the opportunity to see their work as the product of more than a generation of minority advancement as Karl Soehnlein does with gay fiction, or of blended cultural affiliation as Stephanie Elizondo Griest and Vivien Mejia do. They didn't have to argue for its continued relevance as one part of a reader's vast multimedia diet as Tom Bissell has in his essay on literature and video games, or as Meghan Daum does in her piece about the new "literary" sensibility of public radio. Nor did they conceive of their books and themselves as part of the worldwide exportation of American culture as Nell Freudenberger had to when asked, at twenty-eight, to give a series of lectures about her debut novel at six universities in China.

If the essays in this book are any indication, something is happening just below the waterline of American literature and moving quickly toward the surface. Social trends are locking into place that show reading still can have a vibrant, active place in our cultural lives. Some examples include:

1. Digital communication: Arguing that youth are neglecting reading in favor of online media ignores one simple fact: The Internet is fundamentally a reading and writing medium. Whereas twenty years ago, instantaneous communication meant picking up the phone, now it means typing an e-mail, an instant message, or a blog post. The number of blogs and online diaries worldwide reached 5 million this year, with half their creators under the age of thirty. Say what you want about the contents. That's millions and millions of young people writing and reading regularly out of habit.

2. Online conversation: Each day, reading and publishing are more vigorously debated online than anywhere else in the old mediascape. Book-based weblogs like Bookslut (www.bookslut .com), Maud Newton (www.maudnewton.com), and the e-mail newsletter *Publisher's Lunch* are quickly becoming indispensable reads for the involved bibliophile. Online reading communities like Readerville.com have memberships in the thousands. This number may seem small compared with, say, the weekend traffic at AOL, but it hardly seems indicative of the Web dealing the death blow to interest in books either.

3. The *McSweeney's* Factor: Whatever your opinion of Dave Eggers and his projects (*McSweeney's* and *The Believer* magazines, *The Best Non-Required American Reading* series), I recommend dropping by his next event in your area. See how many of the attendees are old enough to rent a car. Using hip graphics, a laserlike eye for talent, and an overarching belief that the whole book business takes itself too seriously, Eggers and company have convinced a generation of young, media-overloaded readers that literature is cool. Contributors to this anthology like Dan Kennedy and Paul Collins got their start writing for the early issues of *McSweeney's* and its companion Web site, which brought their work to my attention. Mr. Eggers also runs 826 Valencia, a literary arts and education center in San Francisco that provides tutoring, reading groups, and scholarships to school kids interested in literature. The program and others like it are expanding to cities nationwide. And if you believe satire is the last signpost of success, Robert Lanham's essay "The McEggers Tang Clan" pays tribute to this movement.

xviii   *Introduction*

4. Hip-hop America: Hip-hop is the most influential popular music of the last two decades and, not coincidentally, the most lyrically dense. Its influence can be felt in the explosion of interest in spoken word poetry, in new African-American imprints at major publishers, and in the fledgling sector of hip-hop literature. At its core is the symbiotic pairing of "beats and rhymes," of rhythm and poetry. An entire generation of young people, who might not find their writer's voice in high school English classes, are finding it in hip-hop lyrics and spoken word performances. Contributor Paul Flores, a novelist and spoken word artist, works a day job educating high school students through these art forms. Nineteen-year-old Nico Cary, whose poem closes this book, is a former student.

5. Culture of collaboration: In his essay, novelist Adam Johnson makes a modest proposal that writers could stand to work together. Kelley Eskridge and Nicola Griffith, novelists and a couple for nearly two decades, collaborated on their essay, exploring the nature of two writers in love and the intersection of their creative orbits. Across America, their peers are taking this collaboration one step further. Events like the 215 Festival in Philadelphia, Info Demo in Atlanta, the Little Gray Books Lectures in New York, and Book Punk in Austin are putting writers on the same stage with jugglers, fire dancers, radio producers, and punk bands, with gloriously raucous and standing-room-only results. The operating principle in each of these events is juxtaposition and collage. We live in a time of comedians covering political conventions, of musicians in corporate boardrooms, of salons, remixes, mash-ups, of all culture on shuffle and slamming up against itself. Rather than getting lost in the mix, books and writers have an opportunity to

become a vital part of it. If musicians can act, if filmmakers can write books, if DJs can score cartoons, why can't authors play in these sandboxes, too? It can only help level needless cultural hierarchies that make the world of literature an island off the shores of popular culture, instead of a bustling province on the mainland. Put another way, why don't we take the title "writer" as a gateway to hundreds of avenues of artistic possibilities instead of limiting ourselves to books?

6. Culture of transparency: From reality TV to *Inside the Actors Studio* to filmmakers blogging their shooting schedules, we live in a culture where we expect the creative to be visible. We expect the life and process of artistry to be laid out for us (not like author Michelle Richmond's, in her essay about her naughty years as an MFA student), explained without our having to ask. We want liner notes, DVD commentaries, e-mail dispatches from the tour. The book is no longer an end in itself, stresses memoirist Tara Bray Smith in her essay, but a jumping-off point for our physical, emotional, and spiritual interaction with the world it came from.

Put another way, the audience isn't just listening. It's watching, commenting (as Glen David Gold notes hilariously in his essay about googling oneself), and expecting as much as artists can give them, probably more. Though this elevated level of interaction is undoubtedly more difficult for writers—an introverted lot compared to, say, comedians—it's also a golden opportunity to reach over the wall and embrace this new closeness to readers, to mobilize it as author Chuck Palahniuk has done with his street teams, to celebrate it as Jennifer Weiner has done with her enormously popular blog, or to simply enjoy this deepened sense of connection readers now expect from authors. That might scare the pants off writers not accustomed to leading their own fan clubs, but it's where we've arrived as a culture (ask Tracy Chevalier). Those who hide from it do so at their peril.

7. Culture of story: Listen to Steve Jobs talk about the latest offering from Pixar, the creators of the Myst video game series and musical epics like the Flaming Lips' *Yoshi Battles the Pink Robots* and Jay Z's *Black Album*. Their creators all say that, no matter how flashy the effects, in the end it's all about story: A compelling narrative, an original voice, and characters both relatable and wondrous. We writers are the frontline artisans of story. It's our world out there, no matter how humble and plain our creations seem in comparison.

I divided the book into four sections, which I hope will serve not only the essays but different families of readers. "Beginnings" looks at how the writers in this collection came to literature as both calling and career, and is inspired by novelist Christian Bauman's essay "Not Fade Away," about writing as a young soldier stationed in Somalia. "The Life" picks over the grease and spare parts of being a writer and how it's as much a job (as journalist Ben Nugent underscores in his essay) as an art. "The Now" takes on many of the big issues facing us as readers and writers. "The Future" gives us a notion, a great one, about where we are going.

Taken to their logical extent, the ideas here point to a world of possibility for the future of books. If writers may begin their careers online and in live performance instead of the freshly scrubbed halls of the Ivy League and MFA programs, imagine what that will do for American literature's diversity and elitist reputation. If technology was seen as instrument instead of necessary evil, imagine readers downloading reviews and events calendars in wirelessly linked bookstores as they browse, and social software allowing readers to trade books in virtual swaps. If book distribution can be reimagined as *McSweeney's* has done, how far must we be from barrels of lendable books in hotel lobbies, bus stations, coffee shops, and on subway platforms? If authors like David Sedaris, Michael Chabon, and Alice Sebold can fill auditoriums across the country, how soon before readers feel the same attachment to their favorite writers and books as they do to their favorite bands? Most important, how can we make this happen and when do we start trying?

I don't know if many of these dreams can become real given the cold hard business truths of publishing, but I do believe this collection is an invitation to think big. Taken individually, these essays say that this is not our parents' age of literacy. Together, they argue that the sky is not caving in on American literature. Instead, it is opening above us, and in that unknown lie infinite possibilities. That opportunity reminds me why I started this book in the first place: for the challenge, for the vision of a brighter future, and because living a literary life in the morning of the twenty-first century is more fun than anything else I've ever done.

Bookmark now. We're about to begin the next great story.

Kevin Smokler
San Francisco, California
October 2004

PART ONE

. . .

BEGINNINGS

NOT FADE AWAY

Christian Bauman

I'd be hard pressed to tell you exactly what I did in the war—ten years gone, and it fades, man, it fades—but I can still tell you what I read there.

Most of my time in Somalia was spent outdoors, shirtless and sweating in a dusty white-hot port compound near the southern city of Kismaayo. But the end of my tour—a week? two? it fades, man, it fades—was spent in a cramped, second-floor room in the port's headquarters building, awake all night, every night. There was a radiophone on the room's only table; it rang every few hours. My mission was to take a message.

I'd requisitioned a folding chair but it was so uncomfortable I skipped it completely and took to the floor, stretched out with a book on the gritty concrete. I would stand every half hour, wiping dust from my pants and concrete burns from my arms. I couldn't leave the room for more than a few minutes at a time, but I'd step into the stuffy, dark hallway lined with sleeping staff soldiers, boots peeking out from under the

poncho liners they used for blankets. Down to my right the
open door of an office and a constant, quiet conversation in
French: my Belgian army equals, two of them minding the radio in there over a stack of *Penthouse* magazines. They never
stopped talking, those two. Perhaps they worried what might
happen if they did. To my left, the offices were all as dark as
the hall, almost everyone sleeping. There was an American
colonel at the end of the hall, and he watched CNN on satellite all night. As far as I could tell, it was his job.

I read a small pile of books in that little room—long hours
pregnant with time to kill—but only one left an impression,
Hemingway's posthumous *Garden of Eden*. It's a joke to say I
read Hemingway on these nights, in Africa, away to war. They
should take away my writing license for saying such a thing. It's
a joke.

But not really. I didn't know it was a joke. Instead of college I'd studied dishwashing (among other ineffective ways of
attempting to support a young family) before finally giving up
to join the army. I was twenty-two years old in Somalia, but
still a year shy of reading *A Farewell to Arms* and *For Whom the
Bell Tolls*. I'd read "Old Man at the Bridge" and "Soldier's
Home" in high school but was three months shy of reading
them again and understanding.

So I read Hemingway at 2 A.M. in an African war zone,
blameless and innocent, as reading should be. It was a hardback of the first printing of *Garden of Eden*, with a torn jacket
and $1.00 sticker. My mother bought it at a library sale and
mailed it to me along with a pound of beef jerky and film for
my camera. I was twenty-two and didn't know anything about

anything, about this novel and its place in the scheme or Hemingway himself or who thought what about this or that. None of it colored me as I opened the cover and cracked the spine, nothing shading my view as I read the front leaf then the back then the copyright page then the first sentence. The first sentence became the second then the third then it was just me and David and none of that other stuff, just me and the story. They were on the Mediterranean coast and the quiet, sad tale unfolded in colors of salt and white sky with a mouthful of dark wine and sharp, strong marinated olives. David was remembering Kenya and just months before I'd been where he'd been, briefly, and now his world was falling apart and oh I'd been there, too. He would swim and fish in the sun and I would stretch, washing down a stale MRE cracker with a cup of cold coffee, wiping my mouth and listening to the French whispers down the hall then finally back on the floor to my place on the page.

An hour before sunrise the singsong of Somali chatter would float through the window, men brought in from the city to sweep up around the pier. There'd been violence—mysterious and malicious pipe bombs and road ambushes—and within two weeks the Somali men wouldn't be allowed in port anymore. But I'd be gone by then, in Mogadishu with what was left of my unit, then home. For now, though, I was here, in my little night room with a radiophone and a book. The Somali voices meant I had only an hour left on my shift and I would mark my place and close the novel, lighting a cigarette and thinking about what I'd read. When my cigarette was done I'd step down the hall and wake the two Belgian privates. They always fell asleep but knew I'd come and warn them before sunrise. I don't know what they did after I left.

• • •

The army isn't where I started writing, but it is where I started writing well (or, at least, consistently). Back then, most of my writing took the form of poetry and lyrics—I fancied myself a latter-day Woody Guthrie—and there is a clear delineation right around 1991 when I joined the army. Not everything I wrote before I was twenty-one sucked, but if I did something well when I was nineteen it was an accident. It was around twenty-one, twenty-two years old that I acquired a steadier grip on my pen. If I wrote something worth keeping I could look at it and know why, with some idea maybe how to do it again.

I wrote in notebooks, thin-lined five-subject my book of choice but it didn't really matter. The battery maintenance log of my LCM mike boat had a hard, green Government Printing Office cover and thick blue-lined pages; I ripped out the battery-acid test results and filled the book with a mostly true story of a Somali trading boat we almost blew out of the water and the old wrinkled woman who glared unblinking at me from her seat on the ship's bow.

I had an odd style of longhand writing. Notebook open to a spread of two pages I would start on the right page, fill it, then go backward to the left. Like much of what I've done in life I'm not sure why I did this (yo man, it *all* fades). Trying to get at something, I guess. Maybe thinking if I sneaked up backward I could surprise it—grab, capture, and hold it.

There aren't too many examples of this backward prose in my old notebooks, though. Longhand lyrics across two pages are one thing. Seven, eight, twenty pages of a short story are something else altogether. I have careless, impenetrable handwriting and a lazy streak. But there were things and people I wanted to write about that just wouldn't fit within my songs anymore—the casual, creeping nerves pushing a young GI to want to shoot an old woman on an unarmed sailboat. I wanted to write about the soldiers around me, these laughing, spitting, often-silent friends of mine, and about what made them anxious in Somalia and what made them anxious in Youngstown, Ohio. There was a song or two there, but how many songs are you going to write about the same thing?

Back at Fort Eustis, I bought a pack of the cheapest paper they had at the PX and began typing.

• • •

The world of reading truly opens in your twenties. Smart kids can get a lot out of books—I was a smart kid, although brick-stubborn and careless in many things—but you don't *really* get it until you've had to crawl through the mud a few times. Literature simply becomes richer after you've been fired, rejected, stranded, or had to change a few midnight diapers.

The upside of my uneducated situation was that the reading I did in my early twenties, this opening up of understanding, was unencumbered by anyone telling me what not to read or what something really meant or what a prick so-and-so had been to his wife et cetera. There is a downside to this, of course: I'd be hard-pressed to deconstruct *The Recognitions* for you, and there are slices of literature I missed entirely and am still catching up on. Harold Bloom weeps for me.

But I read the later stories of Raymond Carver and the early stories of Annie Proulx for the first time when I was twenty-three, and I didn't need anyone to tell me the work was brilliant and I didn't need anyone to tell me why: The anatomy was there for the dissecting if you were willing to do the work. I didn't need anyone to explain what these stories did to me, how they could make me laugh out loud or sometimes go pale and glance over my shoulder.

Here's another thing: Not many creative-writing professors would have told me Stephen King's *Rita Hayworth and the Shawshank Redemption* is a perfectly built book (it is) or that one should reread Anne McCafferey's *Dragonriders of Pern* as an adult (you should) or that there is something crucial for all young writers in the crime novels of Dashiell Hammett (oh, yes).

I was an enlisted soldier, a private first class when I deployed to Somalia. The young officers, second lieutenants, were about my age. They'd been ROTC, for the most part, meaning they were college graduates. And I wonder, if I'd walked in their shoes, had their experience, would I have read Hemingway in Africa, away to war?

Here's the thing about clichés: They're not clichés if nobody tells you. They're not clichés if you don't know it. And if it is a cliché and you know it, maybe you don't pack it, maybe you don't bring it, and then just imagine what is lost. So much is lost.

• • •

There's a funny line I read somewhere about writers. I can't remember who said it or whether it was about MFA programs or writers' retreats or what, but the gist was young writers learn never to sleep with someone they think isn't as good a writer as they are. Which draws a picture of an aching, hopeful twenty-something presenting a stunningly executed turn of phrase at the door of their intended paramour. Do you look shyly down as they scan your material by candlelight? Do you carelessly, carefully expose a nipple in hopes it might draw attention from your clumsy words?

When I was twenty-two, I slept with—well, never mind. It's not your business. Besides, ten years gone and it fades, man, it fades.

When I was twenty-two, the person I slept with most—as in the same room, not a shared bed—was my barracks roommate. His name was Derek, a squat, dark kid of twenty from a dying trailer town in western Massachusetts. He was two years younger but had been in the army two years longer. As he put it, he skipped the whole "trying to make it in America" thing and reached right for the government's dangling carrot. He mocked me for working minimum wage so long before calling a recruiter.

Derek and I shared our small room, the beer in our refrigerator, a TV, and, for a while, a girlfriend. Derek's collection of paperbacks was the only one in the barracks rivaling mine in size—he favored true-crime and serial-killer books. Derek drank to excess, ate to excess, fucked to excess. He liked to pick fights, whether or not he had any chance of winning. If he'd picked a fight with me he would have easily won, but we never fought. Nobody liked him but me. I didn't like him at first either but was forced to live with him and deal with him. He was a pig, but, you know, I like pigs.

Once a week or so I'd come back to the room and Derek would be gone for the evening, out drinking with friends he'd served with in the Azores. This meant a few precious hours of time alone with my typewriter. He'd stumble in drunk at midnight, spit-slurring questions after he fell into his bunk.

"What're ya doin'?"

"Writing."

"What're ya writing about?"

"Stuff."

"What for?"

No answer.

I never answered this question. I didn't know how to answer it—whether asked by him or anyone else—and was embarrassed. It didn't matter; Derek usually passed out at this point in the conversation. One night he didn't. One night he lay silent a few minutes, then added, "You ever write about me, I'll kill you."

Needless to say, I wrote about him.

• • •

A few years later, silly drunk in a bar with a group of writers one night, I slam-fisted and harrumphed indignantly that I'm just not interested in ivory tower writers—writing from within the towers or writing about them. But that's a naive, simple statement and doesn't quite capture it. Nor is it even really accurate. Lorrie Moore, it could be argued, frequently writes about lives inside the ivory tower, writes from inside the ivory tower, yet her books rest happily on my shelf, spine-cracked from second and third readings.

And what is this tower anyway? Academia? If so, such drunken harrumphs cast this son-of-a-multidegreed-couple as a hypocrite, my own lack of credentials aside.

Or maybe the modern tower isn't academia anymore, but a darker tower, the Manhattan-centric world of publishing and publicists and journalists and media—the strange world where all of writing and literature is simultaneously taken far too seriously and not seriously enough.

You see, it's impossible.

Whatever it is, this tower is an easy target for a riled drunk, but not an actual problem in modern American literary fiction any more than it's an actual entity. The problem is those who holler from their towers with nothing to say. And those who claim to own language and literature the way political conservatives now claim to own patriotism. It comes across in the odd, modern misperception that you can't write unless you went to school for it, and the entwined, blind, twin misperception that if you went to school you can write. James Wood wrote recently, "For the first time in history, many poets and novelists are graduates of English studies," and some of these graduates have grabbed the reins of ownership as if it were a birthright.

But writers and writer programs and oh lordy we don't need to go down that road again. Whether 'tis nobler to write from the tower or from the corner of the pub? To suffer slings of snobbery? Or arrows of my reverse snobbery?

• • •

But just between us, can I admit *The Believer* magazine puts me to sleep? Is that all right? I don't mean anything bad by it, just that sometimes I get sleepy. I've enjoyed books by the majority of the writers involved with the publication. I've enjoyed the first fourteen or twenty-two pages of almost all the articles I've read in there. I like where the Believers are coming from, editorially, and why. But still; new episode of *Venom ER* on Animal Planet or new issue of *The Believer*? My word. Decisions.

They did have a point, though, didn't they, those Believers, with their opening salvo and critical call to arms Sure enough. And although this wasn't their point, it bothers me, yes it does, let me say here: Writing is the only art form where a good number of the artists make a slice of their living criticizing one another in print, in public. Worse, some don't even make their living at it; some do it free of charge.

Actors don't do this. Painters don't do it. Musicians don't. It's weird, it's cannibalism.

• • •

Reading taught me how to write (I'm hardly the first to say this), although I didn't know it at the time. A sort of osmosis; the writers in the audience know what I mean. Reading was a joy, a desperately needed escape—I didn't read to learn, I was reading to read. Still, it slipped through, the crinkled, incomplete spelunker's diagram of how this all works, how to get in, how to get out. Reading wasn't all I needed to be a writer. It wasn't enough, but it was close. Ninety percent of writers' makeup lies in their reading. If I never wrote another word but kept reading, I would become a better writer. Yet if books became illegal for me but my fingers still typed, my artistic progress, I'm sure, would halt.

I am of that Anne Fadiman genus *readerus compulsivus*, and I still read mostly for joy, for discovery, but now I also intentionally read to learn, to hone craft, to keep me sharp, yes. And to keep me honest.

I revisit books I haven't seen since I was fourteen and would crawl through my bedroom window into the humid night, out on the roof over the porch, smoking crumpled, bent cigarettes and reading by flashlight. But now I read these mangled Penguin and New American Library paperbacks the way a young art student in Rome might for the first time walk galleries and cathedrals. I've seen these paintings before, fallen in love with them long ago, but now I carefully eye weight, color, and brushstroke. I've read—in some cases almost memorized—these books before but now I read them again, slowly, to discover why they work (and discover, sometimes, the blemishes I'd missed).

I read my contemporaries now. Someone born directly in the year of my birth always gets my attention; I'm fascinated when all that separates is individual experience. Someone younger than me—I admit, I'm suspicious. Someone on the older end of my generation, or beyond—even more suspicious.

But all just a moment's fleeting thought, with book in my hand, eyeballing the cover, the blurbs, the acknowledgments. Truth is, once narrative rolls I am forgiving. I am as forgiving and as eager as I'd hope a reader would be with me. I am excited, more often than not. At the least, I am curious—curiosity alone can carry us ten or fifteen pages, yes? At best, I am enthralled.

An interviewer once asked Peter Straub something about reading his contemporaries, and although I can't quote it exactly I'll never forget the metaphor of his answer. He said, *Even as a reader I'm a writer—I know what you're doing. But still, I read because I want to see how well you can dance.*

We've all embarrassed ourselves on the dance floor. I have. Moves and steps God never intended the body to make, or dancing partners never selected in the light of day. Worse, perhaps both.

But I love to dance, I love this dance. The din eventually fades—clamor and gossip, the heat of whatever chamber you've created in whichever tower you live in—and you are left, finally, to dance alone. And you do, because there is nothing else.

I write because there is nothing else for me. Nothing else I'm any good at. Some things I'm passable at—but passable isn't what we shoot for, is it?

When I was ten I named my new dog Harold because Harold was the last Saxon king of England. When I was ten I could name all the kings of England from about Hardecanute on. Even if I wanted to, could I do that now? Of course not—it fades, my friend, and what fades is what's not as important. Or useful.

I write for the same reason I read: because it's all there is for me. It would be easy and tempting to say I write to keep things from fading, and I suppose there's a partial truth to it. The bigger truth, though, is I write because it's all that holds me, all that doesn't fade for me; not yet anyway.

I can tell you what I did in the war but it might or might not be true, because I might or might not have to make it up.

Not because I'd intentionally stretch and brag, or because of Tim O'Brien's elusive, slippery war truth, but simply ten years gone and man I'm starting to forget.

But it's funny, isn't it, I remember what I read there. And I remember what I wanted to write; that I had something I needed to say, and—fearless, reckless, naive—scribbled my way toward saying it.

LOOK THE PART

Pamela Ribon

There's something fascinatingly awkward about an author photo. I'm drawn to those glossy shots in the back of books, mostly because the subjects never look all that happy to be there. The authors often resort to clichéd poses, hands on hips, or arms crossed protectively in front of their chests, backs pressed against brick walls in random alleys. Some authors choose the full-body shots—sitting in chairs with their legs crossed, glasses off and in one hand, as if about to correct your latest slip of speech. Their bodies may read confidence, but in their eyes you can see the unnerving fear of having their faces on something they wrote. Forever. It's full exposure.

Some authors' faces read apologetic; all raised eyebrows and crooked grins. They're leaning forward on their elbows, hands under their chins, like this whole thing has been a happy accident. Some authors come across as friendly, familiar. She'd be fun at a karaoke bar. He'd let you borrow his DVDs. I love the photos where they're laughing, admitting to us they don't know how the hell they got here either. I used to stare at these pictures, wondering if there's something universal in what a writer is supposed to be.

The image in my head of a writer is from the summer I was ten years old. I see my father hunched over his electric typewriter, a cigarette burning by his side. He's muttering a sentence to himself, shaking his head, deciding on the perfect participle. Dad had lost his job that year and we were living off my mom's desk clerk wages. We had recently moved to Texas, and when Dad couldn't find any work, he took it as a sign that he was supposed to start his writing career. He probably thought it was more like reviving it, finally putting his English degree to good use.

That's how this story always goes, right? It begins with unemployment. A string of bad luck drives pen to paper, he churns out a few stories, blah, blah, blah. . . . . . nobody thought it would sell . . . blah, blah . . . *Harry Potter.*

Our kitchen was littered with sheets of typewriter paper, smudged and half-finished, a single typo rendering the entire page worthless. A well-worn *Writer's Digest* was always resting at the foot of Dad's writing chair; rejection letters piled in a stack underneath his typewriter, a reminder at the end of the day that he should go back to the real world.

I remember watching him pace from typewriter to couch, mulling some story in his head. He was growing Jack Nicholson's facial hair from *The Shining,* all the while developing an addiction to daytime game shows. All objects were in danger of becoming ashtrays—breakfast bowls, mugs, bottle caps. I think he was starting to scare my mother. To me he seemed like the coolest guy on earth. He'd walk circles in our living room, his hands folded behind his head, his eyes staring at the ceiling. There he was, walking and *thinking*. You could just see him *thinking* like that, deep in his head.

There were all these sounds that would come out of him, by-products of deep, intense thought. My favorite was one he'd use when the word he was searching for started forming in his head: "Yud-da-duh-da-duh-da-duh." My sister was a fan of the slow, quiet curse word. He'd start with "Sh." Aware that there were young children present, he'd hold that sound for seconds, flipping through stacks of paper, searching through folders and files. We knew if we waited long enough, our patience would be rewarded with a whispered "-it." Sometimes he'd exhale this huge puff, like there was never going to be another sentence written on this planet. All the words were taken.

That's how my father wrote three short stories that summer. One was about our cat getting out, and how guilty he felt for spending an extra minute going back into the house to put on his sneakers instead of running out into the street to find my beloved feline. He sent that story to *Cat Fancy*, and when they turned it down, Dad threw the rest of the copies into the trash. A story about a poker game went to *Playboy*, and I remember how ashamed I was that my father had to write smutty short stories to put us through public school.

That was also the summer I wrote my first short story. I got a clunky, old, forty-pound typewriter at a garage sale. I put my pillows on the floor of my closet and taped pieces of paper to the walls, notes that read, "Deadline THURSDAY!" or "LUNCHROOM. IDEA??" I stared at the ceiling. I paced the length of my bedroom. And then I decided to do what every writer does in his or her first attempt at greatness: I ripped off my favorite author. I wrote a two-hundred-word horror story about a limb-eating monster worthy of a cease and desist from Stephen King. Mom thought it was brilliant, because she's my mom.

But I didn't want to be a writer; I wanted to be a doctor. Or a lawyer. Something smart that required a Harvard education. Meanwhile, I was writing constantly. In order to stave off boredom, I wrote notes in every class to friends. By the end of junior high, I had memorized over fifteen different origami-inspired ways to fold love notes. On a dare I once wrote a 205-page letter. I filled a Mead notebook in one weekend just to see if I could do it. In high school I wrote a very bad serial comedy detective story that made absolutely no sense. I'd write a chapter at night, and the notebook would be passed around in school the next day. I'd get it back at the end of the day and write more. "You've gotta write another chapter," a complete stranger would say to me, stopping me in the halls between classes. I killed off my main character one month later, a little freaked out by the attention.

I threw away any notion of a retirement fund by deciding late in high school that I wanted to be an actor. My eleventh-grade English teacher encouraged me to keep writing, submitting my essays for contests, while giving me additional writing assignments. He didn't know I was turning in only a very small fraction of the writing I was doing. I was filling journals with stories and poems, but it was rare to find one not focused on a girl pining over yet another boy.

In college, a directing teacher complimented me on the journal I kept while working on a scene. "I really think you should focus on your writing," he said. "You have a talent there. It's tough to be an actor."

"Thanks," I said. But all I could think was *"You're saying I'm ugly."*

Along came the Internet and with it a new way to pretend I wasn't a writer. I'm convinced inspiration comes from someone else's asinine comment. For me the dumb-assery can be attributed to my boyfriend at the time. When I asked how I could start my own Web site, he smirked, "Um? I don't think so. The Web's not for girls."

I immediately taught myself HTML and started writing online. A few years later, while working in a cubicle, I began writing what used to be called an online journal. Before that it was called an Internet diary. Today people call it a blog. Pamie.com (or "Squishy," as it was nicknamed) was where I wrote stories about my life—anything from what a stupid thing I did at work to how my cats were feeling about the most recent change in their diet. Friends didn't understand why I would write about my private life for the world to read. But what they really couldn't understand was why people were reading it.

Truth be told, I couldn't either. At the time I was working hard to use my acting degree to its fullest, performing five improv shows a week at the local comedy club in addition to doing the occasional play. I was working tech support for a major computer company. I used my Web site to land a few freelance writing jobs, but as far as I was concerned, I was no more a writer than I was a Web designer. It was something I did for cash while trying to catch an acting break.

I started Pamie.com in order to look as if I was working when I was sitting at my desk trying to avoid working. This was during the glorious dot-com years when most of us were paid right out of college for jobs that didn't require a full day's work. We became experts at covert operations: Web surfing, office supply swiping, or (in my case), sending out thousands of electronic words like messages in bottles, hoping someone would hear me and respond.

People soon did, in the form of fan mail. The first piece felt like pure celebrity. A complete stranger had taken the time to write, saying, "I feel the same way" or "You're hilarious." I instantly imagined those old post office sacks of mail arriving at my front door, stamped, "Pamie.com. URGENT!" A kid with a heavy sack on his back and a newspaper boy hat: "Special delivery for you, Miss Ribon!" Me in something pink and silky, a long cigarette dangling from between my fingers as I read through the latest from my adoring fans: "*Oh, be a dear and throw them with the others, would you?*"

I wrote more and more, addicted to the instant feedback, delighted with myself for turning my office computer into a virtual pen-pal machine. By the end of my first year writing online, I had the electronic version of my post office fantasy. I received hundreds of letters a week from people sharing their own stories, asking questions about my private life, requesting to see other things I'd written. I was a secret celebrity, a name known in less than five hundred households. At the time I didn't know anybody else who was writing online, creating an audience. With no way to measure my success, I had no idea what to do with it.

The online diary community was small back then, and word about a great new journal would travel fast. It took links from only two of the more popular sites to triple my readership. I was asked to join a Web ring (I just made a bunch of old-school Web people tear up with nostalgia). I attended the South by Southwest Interactive conference, the one place outside San Francisco where web people were considered cool, and took notes. I decided to use my site as a way to showcase my writing to maybe make a little money. A friend on the comedy scene was a fan of Pamie.com. He recommended it to his coworkers and helped me land a weekly humor column in the *Austin American-Statesman*. You know you've officially become a celebrity when you get your first fan letter from a prison inmate ("Please send pictures").

I submitted sample stories from Pamie.com to other sites I admired and found lifelong friends at Über Interactive, a Canadian husband-and-wife team that published several humor sites. When they created TelevisionWithoutPity.com they asked me to be on the staff. I was creating a portfolio of work, writing for Web sites even if they couldn't afford to pay, trying to create a bio. My query letters were electronic. My *Writer's Digest* was Yahoo.

The next summer South by Southwest Interactive asked me to run their panel on Internet diaries. I convinced a girl-centric Web portal to sponsor my site with ad banners. I received awards from the diarist community, including a Legacy award for being a trailblazer: I was a diarist contractually bound to write in her journal. In just two years after starting Pamie.com, I was getting paid to write full time, with jobs I had acquired through my Web site. I was able to save enough money to quit my cubicle job and move to Los Angeles because that's where actors go.

I was an actor who made a living through writing. I figured it would make me a well-rounded performer, and it certainly gave me the kind of working hours needed for auditions. My Web site audience was encouraging, even coming out to see shows I was in. It was like having a tiny cheering section rooting for me even when I was at my lowest points. No matter what I did, they were still there. I was learning business and computer skills, and every day was another writing lesson. I began to cater the Web site to my readers' desires, selling merchandise, holding contests, telling stories I knew would appeal to them. The immediacy of the feedback kept me writing constantly. And I learned how to write for an audience, how to write dialogue that was entertaining on the page. Or screen.

Pamie.com now had a thriving life of its own. One night two girls were posting on the site's bulletin board at the same time. They got into a conversation and realized they were attending the same school. In trying to determine where they lived in the city, they realized they were both living on campus. They looked out their windows and saw each other's bedrooms from across the quad. They met in the middle of the night at a tree between them. They are best friends today, and I still receive letters from them at holidays.

Inspired by a girl's e-mail, which told me she was new in town and couldn't find any cool people to hang out with, I suggested a Pamie.com Cool Kids Meeting, where readers of the site would meet for coffee. The Austin one was so successful it became a monthly gathering, complete with readings from the members' own journals. The clubs grew, and soon there were gatherings in many major cities. They still happen to this day. Attending a convention comprising people who know an awful lot about my private life is one of the strangest experiences I've ever had. But the readers of Pamie.com have always been remarkably nice, fun, intelligent people who share a love of books, music, writing, and pop culture.

Pamie.com was at its most popular, with several thousand daily visitors, when Dad asked me for some help with his writing: "Hey, I was wondering if you could help me get on that World Wide Web."

I knew he occasionally flipped through my Web site to find out what I was up to. He told me he'd stop reading whenever I mentioned sex or the words *Britney Spears*.

I was happy to hear that Dad was interested in writing again. It had been a long time since that summer of unemployment, and though Dad tried the occasional writing class, he would always get bogged down in what he called the necessary "research," and he couldn't seem to get started telling the story.

"What are you looking to do?" I asked.

"Well, I was reading this article about authors. And it seems that some writers, what they do is they write a chapter or so at a time and post it on their Web site. They post a little more, every day or every week, and people go back to the Web site and read it."

I remember the silence as I slowly lowered my head to my desk.

"Dad. That's what I do."

"No, no," he said quickly. "I mean real writers. They put up a few hundred words and keep updating their Web sites, and people read what they write."

How could I consider myself a real writer when I was sometimes paid in candy bars and glitter makeup? I may have built a T-shirt-buying, Internet-ad-clicking, Web-savvy audience with my bare HTML-novice hands, but I wasn't a real writer. Real writers graduate from Harvard and get invited to those workshops where people quietly bring food to their cabin doors. Writers have their theories discussed in classrooms or *New Yorker* articles. Writers don't talk about their periods on the Internet.

When I lost my Web funding in late 2001, I wanted to do something to repay the audience who had given me the encouragement to relocate and follow my dreams. I felt as if I had a responsibility to those who had been reading me for years, teaching me how to be a better writer. A reader who happened to work for Putnam asked if I'd be interested in writing a novel. I started immediately. My friends at TelevisionWithoutPity.com referred me to their agent. My book started as sample chapters and a proposal. There was doubt that people would be interested in a female-driven novel about the Internet so close to the dot-com bust. Then, on October 1, 2001, I lost all of my jobs and had to go on unemployment. Between faxing my résumé to a hundred different places and applying for every job I could find, I fleshed out the rest of my novel based on my experiences at Pamie.com.

While the book was shopping around, Dad said to me, "I want you to know that it's very hard to sell a novel. You probably won't sell this, but you'll learn a lot."

He didn't want me to go through what he had gone through. He didn't want me to read letter after letter saying I wasn't good enough. I already faced the daily rejection of being an unemployed actor in Los Angeles. Hadn't I suffered enough?

Dad gently reminded me that these things take time: "You don't even have an English degree. Just don't get your hopes up."

"I know, Dad. It's OK. I understand."

We shortened our sentences, making them easier to say to each other.

"Real proud," he said.

"It's 'cause of you."

I wondered how much he remembered the summer he had been a real writer. He didn't know he had caused a ten-year-old girl to fall in love with his idea of the writing process, mimicking it for hours on the floor of her walk-in closet. He inspired me to start writing at such an early age it became second nature, what I did to pass the time.

He became very sick as I waited to hear if anyone was going to buy the novel. In his hospital room, we had a conversation about regrets. "Sure was looking forward to seeing your name on a book," he said. "I hate that I'm going to miss that."

Three months after my father died I sold my first novel. That's how these stories always go, right?

I find myself stopping sometimes in the little moments to wonder what he'd have to say about my life as a "real" writer.

He'd have gotten a kick out of seeing my galleys (and the hilarious mistake of my name misspelled on the spine), tracking the book on Amazon, or watching me read on my first book tour. What would he think of my own writing process? Would he be as in awe of Pamie.com as I am, when I receive letters from young women graduating from college who have read me since they were in high school?

With today's greater understanding of the Internet and blogs, what I do is no longer confusing to people. I don't have to dismiss it as a time waster or a way to make spare cash. Instead, I'm proud of having found a different way to become a writer. And though I'm still a performer, these days I tend to perform pieces I've written myself. I am lucky enough to be able to spend my days writing. When people ask me how I became I writer, I answer, "I started writing at ten and never stopped." My secret is I always sought to make my audience larger. The performer in me helped me start a writing career; the Web geek in me took care of the rest.

There are still days when I pace my living room, crumpled paper at my feet, rejection letters tacked to my bulletin board. If I still smoked, there would be overflowing ashtrays. If I could grow a beard, I would have one. But I no longer have the fear that deep down I'm not supposed to be a writer. You don't get to decide those things. It's not about having a degree or winning a prestigious award or finding a respected mentor. It doesn't have to be about chapbooks and literary journals. How it works now is that if you're writing something someone else is reading, for better or worse, you're a writer. You just have to decide what you're going to do about it. Dad would

have liked that part of it. Takes the pressure off. It allows you
to just write.

In my own author photo, I'm leaning forward, but you can't
see below my shoulders. I'm grinning the same half-smile Dad
had whenever he found something ironically amusing. I bet
the face in my picture says what every author thinks when he
or she holds that first bound copy:

*"Amazing who gets to write a book these days. Guess I'm a real
writer now."*

BORDER LINES

Stephanie Elizondo Griest

I grew up in a half-white/half-brown South Texas town, so my first encounter with literature was—as with most things—racially loaded.

In third grade, my teacher announced that our reading class had too many students and needed to be split. One by one, she started sending the bulk of the Mexican kids to one side of the room and the white kids to the other. When she got to me, however, she peered over the rims of her glasses and inquired: "What are you, Stephanie? Hispanic or white?"

I'd been asked this many times before, but didn't have a ready reply. Both? Neither? Either? Half my roots dwelled beneath the pueblos of central Mexico; the other half were buried in the Kansas prairie. I had inherited my mother's olive skin and my father's blue eyes. *Abuelita* Elizondo stuffed me with tortillas and beans; Grandma Griest fed me chicken-fried steak and mashed potatoes.

Scanning the classroom, I noticed my best friend Melida among the brown kids. "I'm Hispanic," I announced. The teacher nodded and I joined the Mexicans. A few minutes later, a new teacher arrived and led us to another room, where she passed around a primer and asked us to read aloud. I quickly realized the difference between the other students and me. Most of them spoke only Spanish at home, so they stumbled over the strange English words, pronouncing *yes* like "jess" and *chair* like "share."

I had the opposite problem: I spoke fluently in our English-only classroom but stuttered at *Abuelita* Elizondo's. My mother had faced such ridicule for her Spanish accent growing up that she never used her native tongue at home. Even though I lived in Corpus Christi, some 150 miles from the Mexico border, my Spanish had barely evolved beyond "Donde esta el baño?"

When my turn came to read, I sat up straight and said each word loud and clear. The teacher watched me curiously. After class ended, I told her that I wanted to be "where the smart kids were." She agreed and I joined the white class the following day.

For the next eight years, whenever anyone asked what color I was, I said white. And nearly every aspect of culture affirmed this choice of racial identity—especially literature.

My collection started with Beverly Cleary's tales of a girl who baked a doll into her big sister's birthday cake and a boy who delivered newspapers with his trusty dog Ribsy. Gradually it progressed to stories about runaways who slept in abandoned boxcars in the forest and grandiose bedrooms at the

Metropolitan Museum of Art. There were Sweet Valley High twins who roared around sunny California in a convertible, and a girl named Deenie who rubbed her Special Place with a washcloth until she got a Special Feeling. (I sat in my bathtub for hours, trying to find my own Special Place. Was it that spot behind my elbow? Or just beneath my pinkie toe?)

All the while, I wondered: Who *were* these people? Where were their *tios* with their big-ass trucks and their *primos* with their low-riders? How come nobody ever ate *barbacoa* or cracked *piñatas* or listened to Menudo or shopped at HEB?

Although I noticed literature's dearth of diversity at an early age, it didn't occur to me to take offense. I just assumed that white people's stories were more worthy of being told. After all, everyone on TV was white, the characters in my *Highlights Magazines* were white, the singers on Casey Kasem's American Top 40 were white (or black). On the rare occasions Mexicans made a media appearance, they were usually either a housekeeper, a wetback, a *cholo*, or a *puta;* in my Texas history textbook, they bore the sole distinction of murdering Davy Crockett at the Alamo.

And so I began emulating the white girls in my books—rolling up magazines to use as kindling in my little house in the big woods, cutting up carrots for my pet pegasus, and attempting to visualize what my big sister and her friends were doing in her bedroom (where I was forbidden) with my ESP. Though I only visited her once a year, I started relating better to Grandma Griest out in Kansas because she more closely resembled the feisty Jewish grandmothers in my books than *Abuelita* Elizondo, who lived on the other side of town. I used to pump my white grandma for stories about her life on the prairie as she baked me fat vats of macaroni and cheese. When I wound up across the counter from *Abuelita* Elizondo hand-rolling tortillas, however, I'd sit in silence—and not just because of the language barrier. I simply couldn't fathom she had anything interesting to say. Rather, I'd watch her flip the *masa* on the burner and wish she'd whip up something like Are-You-There-God-It's-Me-Margaret's grandma would instead. Like matzo ball soup (which I imagined to be minimeatballs drowning in cheese sauce).

Consequently, I never heard firsthand about how my *abuelo* watched his own father get killed by a runaway mining cart as he waited on the opposite track, clutching his lunch pail, or how his mother then crossed the Rio Grande into Los Estados Unidos by canoe with five centavos and a half dozen children in tow. Entire generations of our family became Kineños—the Mexican cowboys who worked the animals and the land of the legendary King Ranch of South Texas. I learned few of their names and none of their stories.

• • •

My senior year in high school, my guidance counselor called me into her office and asked the same troubling question: "What are you, Stephanie? Hispanic or white?"

Before I could reply, she offered that a Hispanic *H* on my transcript would get me a lot further with college scholarship committees than a white *W*. I agreed to the change and the funding poured in—so much that I enrolled at the University of Texas at Austin free of charge. I was ecstatic—until I actually started meeting "real Latinos" (i.e., those who bore the hardships of their skin color) in my classes. I quickly realized I had reaped only the benefits of being a minority and none of the drawbacks, and guilt overwhelmed me. Had I snatched away scholarships from a *real* Mexican kid out there? If so, what should I do? Give back the money I'd received? Take out a loan? Transfer to a cheaper school?

I resolved instead to become the *H* emblazoned on my transcripts, taking a job at the minority recruitment center at the admissions office, volunteering at Latino public schools, joining Latino organizations. But though UT was home to the Benson Latin American Collection, the largest university archive of Latin American materials in the United States, Latino voices were bizarrely lacking in my classes. In my mandatory "Survey of American Literature" course, we spent four months dissecting the works of Twain, Whitman, Emerson, Thoreau, Hawthorne, Dickinson, James, Melville, Eliot, Poe, and Hemingway. Then, on our final day of lectures, the professor devoted forty minutes to the Harlem Renaissance and ten to the poetry of Adrienne Rich. I raised my hand just before the bell rang and asked about Chicano writers. As everyone gathered their papers and headed toward the door, he recommended I read *The House on Mango Street*. And that was it.

Fortunately, the Chicano professors I later sought out *did* introduce me to the vibrant world of Latino letters—and I had an entirely new cast of characters to emulate. I decorated my walls with images of Frida Kahlo and the Virgen de Guadalupe, slammed tequila shots, ate beans and rice, and got a

Colombian *novio* (bad idea). I changed my white-bread middle name (Ann) to my mother's maiden name (Elizondo) and made everyone use it. I even set aside my liberal views on abortion and gay rights and delved back into Catholicism.

But something stopped me from committing fully to this little cultural excavation. I still had no desire to learn Spanish—perhaps because I couldn't fathom where it would get me besides, well, Mexico. And I had wanderlust. Bad. So rather than study the language that would have enabled me to talk with my dwindling elders, I majored in post-Soviet studies, learned some Russian, jetted off to Moscow, took a crash course in Mandarin, then headed over to Beijing. Between 1996 and 2000, I visited more than a dozen communist and postcommunist nations, where I documented the family histories of everyone I encountered—research that later served as the backbone for my first book. But never did it occur to me to record the stories of my own family on my visits back home to Corpus Christi. I didn't think anyone wanted to hear them.

•   •   •

In August 2000, I joined an eight-member documentary team for a nonprofit education organization called the Odyssey. Armed with laptops, digital cameras, and copies of Howard Zinn's *People's History of the United States*, we divided into pairs, piled into cars, and traipsed a total of 315,000 miles across the country, documenting the histories generally omitted in classroom textbooks—slave rebellions, garment worker strikes, the American Indian Movement—and posting them on a Web site monitored by hundreds of thousands of K–12 students nationwide. Late that autumn, our director sent me to Brownsville, Texas, to write about the legacy of the Treaty of Guadalupe-Hidalgo, the 1848 agreement that forced Mexico, after it lost the war, to cede 55 percent of its territory (including present-day Arizona, California, New Mexico, Texas, and parts of Colorado, Nevada, and Utah) to the United States for $15 million.

I hadn't been that far south since I was eleven. And what I saw shocked me. Portable "Skywatch" towers were manned twenty-four hours a day by armed agents with infrared, thermal-imaging night goggles. Stadium lights illuminated the riverbeds. Electronic sensors detected motion, body heat, and ground radiation. A green-and-white INS jeep roared by every minute; a helicopter, every ten.

I walked across the International Bridge in a daze. Hundreds of Mexicans milled along the banks of the Rio Grande below, hawking rosaries, contemplating their chances of crossing. Just as my great-grandmother had some seventy years before. As I crouched down for a better view, my fingers instinctively curled into a note-taking position. I wanted to talk with them so badly my throat ached. But—directions to the nearest *baño* notwithstanding—any attempt to communicate would have been futile. I had to settle instead for interviews with a white National Park Service ranger and a Chicano university professor, conducting them in the language of the people the treaty had benefited. This shamed me, deeply. I started thinking of the extraordinary citizens I had met during my travels who had bravely sacrificed for their culture: those who had nearly perished in the gulag for printing underground newspapers in their indigenous languages; the Tibetans who had risked death for worshiping their ancient gods. I, meanwhile, had abandoned half of myself long ago. And now I wanted it back.

In some ways, I am too late: All of my elders are dead now. Though I am deeply grateful for the Griest family stories I managed to collect as a child, the history of my Elizondo family is what I am likely to spend much of my literary career recreating. What is salvageable can be obtained only via a very long road, the first leg of which entails a serious study of Spanish; the second, a prolonged stay in Mexico. The thought of doing this terrifies me. If I had never connected with a single soul in Russia, it would have been disappointing—but bearable. In Mexico, it would crush me.

But I realize now that Spanish will give me a greater intimacy with my family, with my culture, and ultimately with myself, and I feel ready to attempt this commitment. As for future writings, I hope to honor those who search library shelves for books that legitimize the strange spices emanating from their grandmothers' kitchens. And to empower them with the stories they have to tell.

THE INVISIBLE NARRATOR

Howard Hunt

My background is magazine editing. I fell into the trade by accident in the late eighties, when I submitted an article to the Australian franchise of *Rolling Stone* in my first year of college. The article was a short, acerbic review of the local bands in Brisbane, my hometown. In my opinion, all the bands except one were total crap. What I neglected to tell the editors in Sydney was that I played guitar in the one non-total-crap band.

To my astonishment, the article was accepted and published without the usual rigors of fact-checking, and its publication kicked off a furious spate of letter writing from the Brisbane rock community. Brisbane was very much a cultural backwater in those days, so the editors of *Rolling Stone* were quite surprised to find themselves on the receiving end of a lot of passionate hate mail from a sleepy northern readership they didn't know existed. To my knowledge, they published every letter.

Then they offered me a job.

At the time, I was studying journalism and law, and I knew next to nothing about magazine writing. What I did know was that I wasn't very good at following rules, and that the "hard news" format of newspaper journalism was extremely rule-based. I had read lots of books as a kid, but following a seminal exchange with my mother ("Don't play the electric guitar, Howard; it's so *common,*") I abandoned reading for guitar practice at the age of fifteen, and for the next three years, the only books I read were rock encyclopedias and biographies, the writing quality of which was sketchy at best. There were some exceptional works of rock journalism out there, but I was interested in information, not technique, so the idea of music writing as an art form didn't really sink in until I was struggling to try to produce it myself.

Needless to say, my early articles were shocking. I blew more interviews with famous musicians than I care to remember, and I learned the dos and don'ts of interviewing the hard way:

> ME (FIRST QUESTION): So Elvis, what do you hate most about journalists?
>
> ELVIS COSTELLO: Fuckin' stupid questions like that, for starters.

But somewhere in the middle of the confusion and excitement, I began to read the long feature articles in the American and British rock press, and it was here that my original love of writing kicked in.

When you think *Rolling Stone* and rock journalism, the original point of reference is Hunter Thompson, but Thompson was a dinosaur in the late eighties. The music writing that was coming out of the States and the UK when I was in my late teens was invariably profile-and-thesis–based, and featured the concept of the *invisible narrator*. Whereas a Thompsonesque piece would deliver thesis in the form of Hunter staggering around in his own articles, ruminating obtusely on the nature of things, the meat of invisible-narrator journalism was delivered via the far more difficult practice of a writer accompanying subjects on some kind of adventure, and giving them plenty of rope to hang themselves with.

In profile-based journalism, "thesis" really only consists of two questions: *Who?* and *Why?* Who is Sting? And why is he this way? The simplicity/complexity of these questions gives a writer tremendous latitude to uncover and develop a thesis, based upon how deeply he or she wishes to probe the subject, combined with the time and access granted by the profile material. Thompson was an outsider, so he wrote from the outside, whereas the real skill of invisible-narrator journalism hinges on a writer's ability to get inside a subject, and get inside fast.

The secret to getting inside a subject is that you need bucketloads of empathy. You need to cross the line between interviewer and interviewee in the first five minutes of interaction and make the rock star in the leather pants understand that *your shit is just as interesting as his.* If you can make this connection, it is then fairly easy to propose some kind of extracurricular activity in which you and your subject can "hang out" and "do stuff." This is the rope. If the magazine you write for is sufficiently high-profile, you will find yourself accompanying David Lee Roth through a bunch of Vegas strip clubs, or shadowing Sting through the Brazilian rain forests, or watching Mike Tyson work his unselfconscious charm in a roomful of teenage supermodels.

And it is here that you disappear.

If the first step is empathy, the second step is invisibility. You get so far inside the profile material that the person you're interviewing forgets you're there. And then the story writes itself. For no matter how hard your garden-variety celebrity will try to project a suave, united front, a public excursion plus ego will unravel it. All the invisible narrator has to do is be unobtrusively on the scene with tape recorder in hand, and possess the kind of analytical mind that can break down the complexities of human behavior.

Invisible narration is technically hard to pull off. Aside from thesis and access, you need to be able to paint a convincing picture of the subject matter traveling alone. It's just the reader and Sting in the rain forest. The writer, like the documentary filmmaker's camera crew, is nowhere to be seen.

Tom Wolfe championed this kind of writing in the sixties, but if you read his famous magazine pieces, he makes the classic mistake of getting bogged down in the reportage. At the end of the day, if you walk into a cake shop, you really don't need to list every cake behind the counter. You're in a cake shop. There are cakes. What makes the cake shop interesting is what the profiled is doing inside it, and whether, through the interaction of profiled and cake shop, we can somehow find the answer to "Why?". More often than not, the answer won't be forthcoming, so meticulous detail won't save you. But interesting stuff goes on in cake shops, and the great thing about the flexibility of the rock press is that you could, if the long-haired gods of insight were to smile upon you that day, bang out a forty-five-hundred-word, entirely cake-shop-based article, nail questions one and two of the thesis, and have the thing published. All without ever using the word *I*.

Invisible-narrator journalism also happens to be a terrific boot camp for third-person fiction writing. I've never taken a creative writing class, but my friends who have go on and on about "fieldwork." Getting out there, watching people, that sort of thing. For me, the big difference between the MFA and journalism schools of writing is that journalists are professionally expected to deliver the *Why?* whereas trainee fiction writers tend to focus more on manner and character. It's one thing to go to a café and take notes on the couple having the argument across the room, but getting up, crossing the room, and saying, "So guys? What's the problem?" requires the kind of intrusive personality that the vast majority of people are not born with. You have to *learn* to be intrusive, and there's nothing quite like an editor/deadline/paycheck to help further the education process, especially if the editor is a monster, the deadline is yesterday, and the paycheck is desperately needed to cover your rent. Walking across the room becomes part of the gig. The fact that the girl is sobbing in staccato, mewling bursts or that an interesting blue vein is throbbing in the guy's neck is beside the point. We want thesis. We want to know who these guys are and why they're fighting. And if there's money on the table and rent to be paid, we'll walk across the room and make them tell us.

If journalists-turned-fiction-writers are steeped in thesis, the question has to be asked: "Where are the great works of fiction by the ex-journalists of our generation?" Thesis, after all, is an important and beneficial part of writing, and is often the make-or-break line between "entertainment" and "literature." The answer, I think, is that journalists are trained to think inside the square, the square being the framework of the publications they write for. If you have a nose for a story, the story will write itself, whereas if you take away the story—if you say, "There is no story, make up a story of your own"—the absence of framework is a source of deep bewilderment for most journalists, as making stuff up goes against their training. You can be the most fabulous wordsmith in the world, but if you want to be a storyteller, you need to have a story to tell. A large part of Thompson's and Wolfe's early success was due to the fact that they broke outside the square (or maybe, back in their day, the square expanded to accommodate them), but if you read their fictive journalism—*A Man in Full* being a classic example—their narrative threads become untethered in the final act, and whatever thesis they were grasping for is buried beneath a lot of hackneyed, last-minute plot resolution.

In my opinion, the most complete novel by a former journalist in recent memory is *Silence of the Lambs* by Thomas Harris, for the simple reason that the story dominates the research, and that the plot, character development, and research are impeccable. Harris is a former newspaper man, so his language is conservative, but he delivers continuous thesis throughout the book, mainly concerning the media's culpability in fueling public fascination with serial killers and death.

For all its brilliance, *Silence* was a straightforward, workman-like novel, and you can tell that Harris was thinking outside the square (story first, reportage second) when he wrote it, in a way that he clearly wasn't when he wrote *Hannibal*. At the end of the day, when you break down the various components of fiction—story, form, technique and thesis—story is going to win every time, but I fiercely believe that the two strong suits of the journalism school, technique and thesis, are the key to the ongoing advancement of literature, and that the present convergence of media is threatening to make them obsolete.

Magazine journalism is not what it used to be. My friends in the business regularly complain that their publications are commissioning shorter and shorter articles, and that the length constraint really challenges their ability to deliver "atmosphere" and "mood." Up to the point where the standards slackened and bikini pictorials became the order of the day, quality lifestyle magazines demanded a lot from their readership. They expected you to commit serious time and energy to reading them, and in exchange for this commitment, they rewarded you with exceptional writing. As a kid reading the great practitioners of invisible narration—Bill Zehme, Chris Heath, Mark Singer, David Kamp, Erik Hedegaard, Jon Savage, Tom Junod (before he went to *Esquire*), Rob Tannenbaum, Lynn Darling, E. Jean Carroll (before she got her TV show), Andy Darling, Jon Wilde, to name but a few—I was sufficiently inspired to sit down and try to replicate the various techniques I could see them using. In the majority of cases, the articles were *long*. To paint a really good picture, you need material and space, space being a rare commodity in the largely visual evolution of magazines these days.

An example: For over ten years, I've carried a sentence from an early *Details* profile of Christopher Walken around in my head. Walken is in a downtown café, giving (almost but not quite) invisible narrator Erik Hedegaard the spooky treatment. The experience has been unsettling, so Hedegaard writes, "Fiddling with his lemons, he seems to repel conversation." Which nails Walken, the interview, the moment in the café. It's an irreverent break, but it works, and the reason it works is that the writer has been given enough space in the article to develop the kind of atmosphere that can accommodate this thought. If you tried to condense an observation like this without the requisite three pages of skillful framing, it wouldn't make any sense. But we've traveled with Walken. We have a sense of his mood. And thus a technique- and thesis-rich sentence is able to convey an uncanny snapshot of a subject in a way that the new trend of big-photo/small-caption magazine journalism cannot.

What I am talking about here is craft. The colorful nature of the celebrity industry really lends itself to colorful writing, and the tangible word length of magazine articles is such that an aspiring writer can sit down and study the craft in bite-sized pieces. But if the pieces become too small, there will be nothing left to study. I'm not suggesting that lengthy feature writing will ever become extinct: The *New Yorker* and *Harper's* and *Vanity Fair* will see to its survival. But the thing is, I wasn't reading those magazines when I was in my late teens. I was reading *Rolling Stone* and *Details*. I was a kid, and in much the same way professional athletes, actors, artists, and musicians develop a love of their profession in their formative years, I fell in love early with writing, courtesy of a rock and lifestyle press that took itself seriously, and a collection of young writers who strove to make an art form out of magazine journalism.

In terms of my own evolution, I traded rock journalism for sportswriting, sportswriting for editing, and then I jumped ship to fiction and haven't looked back since. But I still read magazines—both on- and offline—and to my eye, the youth end of the market has become disturbingly lightweight. Articles are shorter and tend to be more sensational than insightful, and I'm not seeing much in the way of room crossing and empathetic intrusion. What I am seeing is a lot of blithe conjecture and hip phraseology—"The couple across the room are arguing. The couple across the room are *dorks*"—which is a poor substitute for the hard-won intelligence that thesis journalism can provide.

I'm at an age now where I read the twenty-thousand-word articles in the *New Yorker* as a matter of course (and aspire to writing one or two myself), but I often wonder whether this would be the case had I been born ten years later. I was a magazine worm, not a bookworm, and a sucker for music-driven pop culture of any kind, but if my teenage information sources were Web- or T&A-based, I might have fallen in love with some of the models in the magazines, but I'm pretty sure I wouldn't have fallen in love with the writing.

I would have practiced my guitar instead.

FROM SOMEWHERE DOWN SOUTH TO SOUTH BEACH: RAW TAKES ON THE MFA

Michelle Richmond

In August of 1995, my friend Kate and I made the long drive from Atlanta to a small town in the foothills of the Ozarks, a journey that ended with nineteen miles of winding, two-lane country road called the Pig Trail. Kate drove a twenty-four-foot Ryder Truck, and I followed behind in my faithful Toyota. That night, we didn't stop to sleep. Driving along the Pig Trail, which was enveloped in a kind of medieval mist and bore the stench of thousands of chicken coops, I began to question my sanity. Who leaves a decent job and a bustling city for a quiet hill town in the middle of nowhere, committing herself to four long years of *writing*? And who would be benevolent or naïve enough to hire me after this whole thing was over?

The Pig Trail seemed to go on forever. As dawn broke, sweetly dilapidated farmhouses began to take shape in the fog.

We pulled into town at 5 A.M. on a Sunday morning, exhausted and disoriented. I parked the car on some anonymous street and joined Kate in the Ryder truck. We spent a fruitless hour driving around town looking for my apartment and ended up smashing into a giant oak on the outskirts of campus. The tree was barely injured, just a scar along the trunk and a single low-hanging limb detached. Everyone was asleep, the moon was still bright in the sky, it had been accidental, and we were uninsured; we determined that the tree would live and drove away without notifying the proper authorities. Later that day, after locating my apartment, I drove the Toyota into a ditch and was rescued by a couple of locals in a pickup truck, whom I paid off with a case of Guinness. I would later learn that (a) the going price for a rescue-op was a six-pack of canned Bud, and (b) the tree was registered as a national historical landmark. But that is beside the point.

The point is I should have realized that first day, as Kate and I stood examining the injured tree and later the battered car, that I had embarked upon a path of destruction that would be directed both inward and outward. A kind of creative destruction that I would come to remember as one of the most raucous and ill-advised periods of my life, a time that was both productive and maddening, marked by lots of sex and more alcohol and a few stories thrown in for good measure.

What I remember most vividly about my first year as an MFA candidate are the parties. First came the welcoming party at the home of a beloved bear of a professor, whose backyard contained a little pond in the shade of some big green trees. That's the first time I remember taking my clothes off as an MFA. There we were—a bunch of would-be Zeldas sans the fame and the old family money—frolicking in our underwear in a pond in the moonlight less than one week into our graduate school experience. Then there was a party in a dreary seventies-style housing complex, during which we all went outside and sat in an enormous circle and made out—girl on girl, boy on boy, boy on girl, depending on the way the bottle spun—until the neighbors came out and complained that we were threatening the moral integrity of their young children. There was the all-night brew-pub get-together during which I got deliciously smooched by a handsome professional golfer named Mandy, but I was not quite ready to be a lesbian so I never called her, and from there on out my friend Wade from Texas kept serenading me with the melancholy song "Oh Mandy, you kissed me and stopped me from shaking, but then I sent you away."

I was far from an innocent bystander in all of this. I was, after all, responsible for the body-parts party, just three weeks into the semester, during which I took my guests one by one into my walk-in closet, swabbed a chosen body part with finger paint, and impressed their hands, breasts, thighs, and other anatomical delights onto a huge white sheet. I remember this party well because it was the first time I got a full frontal view of my future husband, a quiet San Franciscan with a disconcertingly beautiful head of hair who was so kind as to allow me to enrobe his most valuable part entirely in violet.

Lest you get the wrong idea, it was not all fun and frivolity. About halfway through the year, I sank into a funk from which I could not seem to recover. Instead of writing fiction, which is what I had joined the program for in the first place, I spent most of my time on the two composition classes I was teaching. Because I was new at teaching and terrified of making a fool of myself in front of a roomful of expectant freshmen, I overprepared and spent many hours each week grading papers. Most of us taught two classes of twenty-five or more students, who were required to write at least six papers per semester, plus revisions: You do the math. In addition to the teaching responsibilities, there was a rigorous required course on teaching composition and a form and theory course. The fiction workshop, which met once a week, tended to get the dregs of my energy, and I wasn't the only one who fell into this pattern. I suppose I went into the MFA expecting some sort of kick-ass writing camp. I got my ass kicked all right, but not by writing. It was the unglamorous rigmarole of academia, combined with my own immature devotion to brew pubs and parties, that ultimately snowed me under.

By December, I had only written one new story, and I was turning in old material for workshop. It wasn't the best way to approach the MFA, but I wasn't alone. I've heard the MFA described as a sort of privileged existence, and while it may be true for those whose parents are footing the bill, it certainly isn't true across the board. I will concede that taking three classes and teaching two is far preferable to working a regular office week, but it doesn't leave much time for writing. Most people go into an MFA with a twofold desire: to become a better writer, and to write a book. While many achieve the first goal, the latter is far more difficult.

To add to the many distractions from writing, I had fallen in love with the San Franciscan—with his Elvis curl and his obscure taste in music and his alarmingly elegant hands—and I did not know how long he would continue to be tangentially involved with his previous girlfriend, who was still calling him daily from California. I was drinking too much, sleeping too little, and experimenting with sex toys I'd never contemplated before. It was in this small town in the foothills of the Ozarks that I discovered such accoutrements as the chastity belt, the cock ring, and the leather strap. I like to think all this added some edge to my writing that hadn't been there before, but it is a common flaw of writers to rationalize everything we do or experience, claiming that it will make us better writers.

By the second semester, I decided that if something had to suffer, it would be teaching rather than writing. So I spent nights at an antique sewing table in my apartment on Garland Avenue, with the enormous gas heater blasting warmth into the rooms, drinking pots of coffee and typing stories on a Mac Duo-dock. My apartment was the top floor of a two-story house, and on several occasions my downstairs neighbor, also an MFA candidate, would come tromping up the stairs in the middle of the night, red-eyed and visibly annoyed, pleading with me in his thick Irish brogue, "Michelle, dear, you've got to take your shoes off." I would glance down at my feet, only to realize with embarrassment that I'd been stomping across the hardwood floor in my clogs. On other occasions the same neighbor would show up in a state of drunken good humor and tell me long, rambling stories, or wash my dishes, or both, and it was on those nights that I felt I was coming pretty close to what a writer's life really was—no glamour at all, no fame or fortune, just a vaguely satisfying sense of communing with other literary types who were as messed up as I was.

The stories I was writing during that time were rife with sex, perhaps because I had not yet learned to separate life from fiction. Once, another student had this to say about one of my stories: "People don't have that much sex. It's not realistic." The night before I had watched a graying fiction writer who suffered from posttraumatic stress disorder perform cunnilingus on a young poet in my bed, while the poet's boyfriend looked on. I considered mentioning that the student in question didn't know much about what was going on after workshop, but it didn't really need to be said, because there were only a couple of folks in the class of sixteen who hadn't seen their colleagues in compromising positions.

I wasn't the only one who brought my extracurricular escapades into the workshop in the guise of short stories. There is something very incestuous about the workshop experience, particularly in small towns where the students tend to spend a lot of time together. It's rather disconcerting to sit around a table participating in a critique of someone else's work, only to realize the antagonist in the story is none other than yourself, and no one present thinks you're a very likable character. Or to hear someone who isn't part of a particular clique— writing programs are breeding grounds for cliques—say, "This could never happen," when half of the people at the table were actually present when it *did* happen. (Which is not to say that "But it really happened" is ever an excuse for bad writing.) I remember submitting a story for workshop (it was called, I believe, "Telltale Signs of Love and Deception") with the sole intent of suggesting to the fellow from San Francisco that I was into him for more than sex, that I might, in fact, be getting attached. He didn't seem to get it, or at least he pretended not to; he has always been a master of subtlety.

Another interesting thing about workshops—more true perhaps of the older, more entrenched programs than their newer, more politically correct counterpart—is that new-fangled notions about student-teacher boundaries tend to fall away. The workshop by its very nature requires that boundaries be overstepped, that students and teachers share themselves to a degree they'd never dream of doing in a traditional classroom. Which is why I wasn't the least bit surprised when one afternoon, after I had arrived to class a bit late to find that there were no more chairs available, the professor suggested that I come over and sit on his lap. It was the sort of place where, if I had taken him up on his offer, it probably wouldn't have caused much of a stir. Another professor used the occasion of a workshop to comment that I (not the story, but the author) was "98 percent sex." To be honest I didn't take offense at the time. I was twenty-four years old, adrift in a town that seemed like a step away from my real life, and in hindsight I can see that I very much played the part of the sexual ingenue. They say what happens in Vegas stays in Vegas, and I felt the same way about graduate school.

Now, however, as an adjunct professor at two MFA programs in San Francisco, where one plays strictly by the book in terms of "fraternizing" with students, I can see just how shocking such exchanges might seem to someone earning his or her writer's stripes in the culturally censored atmosphere of the new millennium. The fact is that writing is a dirty, often torrid affair, and its practitioners are among the raunchiest, liveliest, least reverent of citizens—which is why writers and academia, particularly the proper, politically correct academia of the twenty-first century, make for a strange mix. Hemingway chasing bulls in Pamplona, Fitzgerald drinking himself to oblivion in New York, Oscar Wilde drafting long, revealing love letters from prison—these are personae who somehow match the place and the circumstance. But a forty-something truck driver-cum-writer, a shy housewife, and a tattoo artist (the composition of one of my workshops), cooling their heels in a college classroom, discussing character and theme, can be a pretty odd, if invigorating, spectacle.

Big personalities make for big conflict, especially in the lion's den that is the writer's workshop. While some programs take a kinder, gentler approach to criticism, the fact is that the timid just don't fare well in most writing programs. Sitting around a table for an hour and a half while a roomful of writers—some friends, some enemies—tear one's writing to shreds requires more than a thick skin; it requires an ardent and sometimes completely misplaced certitude that one is indeed a writer, to hell with them all. I remember one workshop during which a nice, dullish girl sat sobbing in her seat while the professor ranted about how she should have never been admitted to a writing program. Imagine applying the workshop system to real life. Once a week, you and your friends meet around a table to critique a chosen member of the group. You spend a few minutes mentioning the victim's finer qualities, and then you launch into a large-scale attack on every little thing you don't like about her. Once the three-hour bitch session is over, you're supposed to go back to being friends.

The mishmash of passionate, narcissistic personalities of varying ages and professions, all of whom share an obsessive-compulsive inclination to write and a poorly hidden insecurity, is what makes MFA programs so interesting. It is also what makes one occasionally feel the desperate need to flee. I remember getting in my little red Toyota late one night, with just a credit card and a bag of Fritos, driving away from campus, and somehow ending up on Route 66. I kept driving until I got to Oklahoma, and when I could no longer stay awake I spent a scary night in a rat motel in an ugly section of Oklahoma City. I had no idea what I was doing there. I'd just felt desperate to get out of Dodge.

And get out I did. The next fall, I transferred to the University of Miami. The man with the Elvis curl had finally cut ties with the ex-girlfriend and was slated to transfer to Miami as well, but during the middle of the summer he accepted a gun-toting job with the government. So in the fall of 1996 I found myself alone in a strange and sprawling city, subletting a studio on the beach and driving twice a week into Coral Gables to attend class. I didn't have many friends. I didn't go to many parties. The university had offered me a generous James Michener Fellowship, which included a tuition waiver and a living stipend, so I had huge, uninterrupted chunks of time to write. Sex was an infrequent affair, as the boyfriend was living in New York City and I knew I had to clean my act up if this relationship was going to work out. That's when I really started to write. I began a novel. It was a very bad novel, full of the supposedly clever asides and inauthentic characters that graduate students are famous for. My professor told me that the novel was bad and I should focus on my stories, but I wanted to sell a book, so I wouldn't listen. Of course, it turned out my professor was correct, but it took two years of writing and several months of rejections for me to understand that.

Despite the lousy novel, I learned an important lesson in Miami: how to be a writer. In my studio apartment on the beach, I finally grew up and embraced a lifestyle which, until then, I had been unwilling to accept: a lifestyle of solitude. The idea of sitting alone in a dirty bathrobe with a cup of coffee late on a Friday night may not be appealing to the throng of hopeful writers crowding into MFA programs every year. Certainly, it is neither glamorous nor lucrative. But I believe that those nights alone with the computer, week after week, month after month, are essential if one wants to write a book.

You hear a lot about folks who go to the Iowa Writers' Workshop and are courted by agents and editors, the twenty-something chaps with big egos and bad facial hair who land a Stegner and a major book deal. What you don't hear about are the thousands upon thousands of hopeful writers who go into lesser-known programs in Idaho and Florida, San Francisco and Oregon, Texas and LA and Alaska, and emerge two to four years later with no more to show for their hundreds of grueling writing hours than a largely unpublishable thesis of one or two hundred pages. Iowa and Stanford aside, the truth is that most MFA candidates will not be surrounded by agents and publishers eager to usher them into print. Most will place a story here, a poem there, in reputable journals with limited readership, journals that pay only in copies. And most will watch years, if not decades, pass between the time the degree is in hand and the first book is accepted for publication.

During grad school, much emphasis is placed on the thesis, but this tends to be an artificial construct; serious writers get better over time, and most folks who take an honest look, a few years down the road, at the work they did in grad school will find it rather sophomoric. The thesis itself is usually full of stories and poems that have been put through numerous revisions and repeated workshop sessions, and not always to the story's benefit. Only two of the stories from my thesis actually made it into my first book; most of the stories were written after the MFA, while I was working odd jobs in Manhattan. No agents came knocking at my door until *after* my first book, a story collection called *The Girl in the Fall-Away Dress*, was published. By then I had a novel to sell, but not one of the agents who contacted me was willing to represent a literary novel burdened by what they deemed to be the commercially undesirable theme of lesbianism. After my second book, *Dream of the Blue Room*, was released by a ballsy independent publisher who didn't care that the book wasn't commercial, it was easy to get an agent, but the ease factor ends there. I've never made enough money from writing to take a semester off from teaching, and because I can't imagine living anywhere other than San Francisco—where tenure-track jobs are scarce and you can't walk into a coffee shop without bumping into a published author—it is likely that I will continue to piece together teaching gigs from one semester to the next.

There wasn't a single person with whom I went to school, who didn't have big dreams: we would publish much-celebrated novels, we would win awards, our names would be remembered. A few of us decided that we would pool the proceeds from our first novels to buy some cheap land and a big house in the country, where we would live together and drink beer and write more books. Perhaps the most fantastical notion of all was that we would write *full time*. Now, ten years later, only a handful of the writers I knew in my two programs (from a list of several dozen) have published books. No one, to my knowledge, is actually making a living as a writer. Many are disappointed, some are visibly depressed, and some just don't care, because the years have taught them that there are more important things in life than publishing. I suspect most of us remember the MFA as an amusing jaunt far removed from real life, one that didn't really get us much closer to becoming writers. To be a writer you have to write—and no academic degree is going to do the writing for you.

So why get an MFA? One reason is the simple comfort of being around other writers in a setting in which writing is taken seriously. Among nonwriters, if you mention that you're a writer, there are two likely responses: (1) "Would I be familiar with your books?" (2) "Oh, I've been thinking about writing a novel myself. What do you think of this idea?" If you answer the first question with something honest but embarrassing like, "Well, I haven't actually published a book yet," you'll get nothing but blank stares from anyone who hasn't been through the humbling experience of submitting work for publication. The second question is simply painful, because unless you can find a graceful way to extricate yourself, you're going to spend the next hour listening to someone who hasn't actually read a novel since high school explain why this one is going to be a best seller. MFA programs provide a cushion from the indifference of the masses, a dreamy albeit temporary barrier between those who are truly interested in literature and those who consider *Chicken Soup for the Soul* a valuable reading experience. Only in an MFA program will your friends and colleagues understand that a handwritten "not for us, but send again" from the editor of the *Green Swamp Review* is cause for celebration.

Some of the folks you meet in your MFA program will become longtime friends with whom you can discuss books and movies and the sadly commercial state of the publishing industry for years to come, and that in itself may be a fair trade-off for a couple of years in school. You might even end up marrying a fellow MFA, a phenomenon which occurs quite frequently. Take for example the guy with the Elvis curl, who is gainfully employed and sleeping permanently in my bed, preparing in his quiet, gracious way for fatherhood. He also happens to be my best reader, the one person who sees everything I write before I send it out.

In addition to providing a community of writers, an MFA program will give you deadlines. In a two-year program, you're likely to take four workshops, during which you will be required to submit a minimum of eight short stories total. For poets, the numbers go up dramatically. All of this work will receive serious, thoughtful reading by a few, if not all, of your colleagues, as well as your professors. Eight stories in two years is a pretty good chunk of work, and if two or three of them are good enough to be published, then you're on your way to something—probably not fame or money, but at least the vague satisfaction of knowing that somewhere inside that insecure, narcissistic, warped head of yours lurk the beginnings of a writer.

So do you need to go to school to become a writer? Probably not. What you do need to do is read and write and read some more. Revise, revise, revise; educate yourself about literary magazines and publishers; send your work out. Take at least one serious workshop in creative writing before plunging yourself into the MFA life. If you decide the MFA really is for you, look for a school that provides at least partial funding so you don't have to mortgage your house or offer up your firstborn as collateral. Then brush off your finger paints, put on your poker face, and get ready for a very weird ride.

PART TWO

. . .

THE WRITING LIFE

WELCOME. GRAB A BROOM.

Dan Kennedy

January 15, 2004

Even though the subtitle I'm about to lay on you sounds like the name of a bad personal power seminar at a Ramada Inn, I will use it. Which is probably fine because the title I put at the top of the page for you sounds like a rehab slogan or a first day on a bad job. But the less I edit myself, the more I get written. Okay, so . . .

YOU WILL GET IT IF YOU WORK FOR IT

You will get your first break. Because the law of the universe seems to be: Pick something you love to do and do it as steadily as a bad habit, for ten or so years, and somebody will want a piece of it. The only catch is that sometimes it takes way less than ten years, and sometimes it takes way more than ten.

"Man, finally!" you will think to yourself.

"Jesus, not bad after all of these years of doing it for the sake of doing it," you'll continue thinking to yourself.

And you'll maybe add a few thoughts like "Sweet, sweet, God above . . . this is going to feel good. Things are going to change now. Make it grande, God. Let's turn this mother out." And then maybe you'll stop talking to yourself and God in this kind of horrible monologue that's a sort of impotent cross between a soft, white suburban teenage gang thug wannabe, a Starbucks-addicted mother of three, and an aging C-list playboy. And maybe I'd have given your character some better lines back there if I had been writing a little more of late. But I haven't been. I'm arguably a little out of practice at the moment when it comes to my writing, because I got that first proverbial break and instead of writing and staying in practice and shape, I immediately and accidentally took a break. And I've kind of been sitting here since. Between books one and two.

March 15, 2004: They Run That *Cops* Show During the Day!

I don't really know why I'm doing this. It's completely lame to be sitting here between books. As a matter of fact, I would kick my ass if I were you. Like these cops on my TV busting in on the malnourished stoner type of guys who are sitting shirtless in La-Z-Boy reclining chairs watching their TV, drinking the tall can of presumably pretty warm beer from an anemic refrigerator, thinking they are too smart and fast to catch. Honestly, come and get whatever has been given to me if I stay as soft as I have been these last eight months or so, because it'll be easy.

April 11, 2004

I don't believe in writer's block—I'm not working up to a big analysis of why one can go for so long without writing. I don't go in for that whole thing of like (Spinal Tap accent in place) "Look, man . . . it's impossible to [insert any form of creative work] right now. I can't do it, and I don't know when . . . [dramatic pause] *or if* . . . I'll be able to do it again, man." I mean, it ain't backbreaking work, writing. And there's no sense in making a precious and larger-than-life practice of it. I think that things like music, writing, filmmaking are all blue-collar jobs, and I think that it all just gets worse and worse the more people try to position themselves or their craft as anything more lofty than what basically amounts to a job in the service of others. One of my all-time favorite quotes about the creative process of writing comes from Neal Pollack: "I don't see writing as some sort of holy act. When the phone rings, I answer it." Having said all of that, it has taken me a month to sit back down in front of this page. Maybe you can't control when inspiration will strike, but there is something to be said for the discipline of showing up so that when it comes around you'll be there waiting.

May 8, 2004: Holy Christ,
This Thing's On and People Can Hear Me

I spent a long time writing in obscurity. You'll spend a long time writing in obscurity. Jesus, Seattle for instance. Moved up there and all I did was write and work to pay the rent so I could write. Five years there, a few years of the same drill before that in Northern California. Then four years in New York doing more of the same. Twelve years isn't a ton of time, relatively speaking, but this seems like it should be easy by now, writing. I think part of freezing up is that it's new and strange to have a lot of people look at your work after years of relative obscurity. And it's not like my book is some huge best seller, not at all. At the time of writing this, it isn't chasing anybody off the top of the charts. It's not even really chasing anybody off the middle or even the bottom of the charts. When it comes to certified supermega selling success, mine is a book that, at best, *hangs out* in some of the same places as books that are on the best seller lists. At the same time, I would be lying not to admit that I've had the surreal experience of seeing my mug in *People* magazine on an airport newsstand on my way out to my first book tour. And in *Entertainment Weekly*, on CNN headline news a couple of times . . . been asked a lot of questions about why/how/when/what it means/why it's funny on tons of radio stations, read a lot of what critics on newspapers across the country had to say good and bad, and last week had an offer come in from a publisher to translate the book into Chinese and make it available at retailers in China, where apparently there has been some demand for it. China? No matter how much I worked for it or hoped for it, it's a little weird to realize that people are actually reading what I wrote down. For me, I think it was a little easier to write thinking that nobody was listening. On the other hand, there are a lot of people out there with more talent than me that would like to have that problem. Damn it, I had not really thought of that until I wrote it in that last sentence. Jesus, that's heavy. Okay, now I think I'm going to freak out about that, too.

Wednesday, July 20, 2004, 1:04 A.M. Eastern

Kevin, the editor of this fine collection, has e-mailed me and asked if my August first deadline would still be feasible. It's seven months since I started this very short piece of writing. I am up late. I have opened a brand-new blank Microsoft Word document. After I close the document that you are reading right now, I will take the new blank document and make it the start of my second book. Even though I tried to be all tough guy about my creative process and the work of writing, I am secretly under my breath asking something bigger than I that I think may reside far above me in the sky or clouds or universe to please let me stop running from the work I get to do. And I wrestle between that line of thinking and my belief that writing is nothing so precious that it needs nine tons of mustered strength, random travel, and a favor from God to approach. So, then, here's the essay about writing. Now for the second book.

A CALL FOR COLLABORATION

Adam Johnson

You know the myth of the young writer: Hands in jeans pockets, he (invariably it's a he) wanders the quais of the Seine before dawn, absorbing the hollow desperation of the city. His collar is up, his cigarette dim, and he stops to pass a bottle with homeless men whose faded French prison tattoos will certainly show up in his novel. The novel in question (about a guy like himself) is written on a roll of bathroom towels in his backpack. He doesn't read, lest reading corrupt his voice, and though he doesn't speak much, he *sees* everything. He's so outside he's inside, which is why his novel will shine the excruciating light of truth back into the souls of average folks. Or he's in an all-night diner outside Seattle, scribbling notes on placemats while salty eggs cool on the plates of truckers. This writer's wearing an oilcloth coat and his novel's about hitchhikers—he thinks it will probably end violently in Alaska. Or perhaps the writer we're thinking of is in the Mission district, something terribly ironic printed on his shirt. His glasses are purposefully thick, and he's somebody who looks so nobody that he's obviously *somebody*. This novel's about the under-belly of the underbelly, and man, it's raw.

Okay, I'll stop there, you get the picture. Unfortunately, some version of this is what inspires many young writers, and I wish it wasn't so. Not that I'm against aggrandizing artists into romantic figures—it would just be nice to have some variety in the models. How about mythologizing "The Generous, Friendly Dude Who Writes Every Single Day" or "That Soft-Spoken Religious Lady Whose Prose Is Dark and Mesmeriz-ing"? Mostly I'm against the image of the writer as a lone, edgy brooder not so much because it's inaccurate but because it's of little use. Writing is hard work, and if anything's true about the process, it's the fact that a good story is hard to find and even trickier to get on paper. What's less romantic than star-ing alone at a blank screen? And edgy? I've changed the cat litter because I didn't know what my characters were going to say next.

The urge to create a fictional narrative is a mysterious one, and when an idea comes, the writer's sense of what a story wants to be is only vaguely visible through the penumbra of inspiration. A good story feels both surprising and inevitable, fresh and familiar. When starting a story, it seems as if there are a million possible first lines and, if things go right, only one possible last one. Eventually, once the tumbling inertia of scene sets in and characters begin to impose their own will on events, the story begins to dictate its own direction. But how to get from nothing to something? With so many elements outside the writer's initial vision—where to open, what to show, where to go—how does the story get from uncertainty to inevitability?

A writer's "toolbox" is one weapon against the unknown. Though the myth of the lone-wolf writer gets much mileage from the noirish struggle with the creative process, most writers arm themselves with a knowledge of narrative tradition and convention. Instincts, even those amped by sangria and Marlboros, can take a story only so far. For a young writer, a grasp of fiction technique—things like perspective, point of view, tense, narrative distance, point of narration, and so on—should be worth way more than a Eurorail pass to Pamplona. Other, less-flashy qualities like patience, endurance, and effort don't hurt either. I'm a pretty big believer in loyalty, and I try to treat my stories with the kind of commitment I'd show real people. The best new story ideas tend to come along just as a current one seems to be foundering, but it would be like cheating on a story to turn my gaze to a tempting new thing. When a writer is trekking through a novel, new story ideas are like those distant mud cities that appeared to Spaniards as bathed in golden light. At times like that the greatest tool is perhaps fidelity.

I'd like to propose adding collaboration to the writer's toolbox, an idea that strikes at the core of popular culture's conception of the writer as a lone saddle man of the literary prairie. Artists collaborate in music, cinema, theater, dance, and so on. *But only one hand can hold a paintbrush or pen*, most people would counter. Writers already work together in many ways—workshops, salons, editors, reading groups—yet true collaboration is considered outside the process. Is that because collaboration is in opposition to where stories come from and how they get on the page, or is it because it threatens our idea of what a storyteller is?

Somehow it's fine for people to collaborate on a musical or an action movie, but the American novel is off limits. *Rabbit, Run* wasn't written by Updike & Sons and *The Joy Luck Club* didn't come from Tan and the Gang. The place where most interaction is seen between writers on their texts is in the workshops of the university MFA programs. Much vinegar is spilled over the "MFA story," which is supposedly competent yet uninspired. By *competent*, it's commonly thought that the writer's toolbox is full, and by *uninspired* it means they've never seen a bullfight. That portrait's just the opposite of our mythic would-be Kerouac, who is highly inspired, yet incompetent. Personally, I believe the proliferation of MFA programs is a good thing—more hounds to the hunt—and what's wrong with learning the skills of writing first, so that when an important story comes along, it has a game author?

Every writer is given a gift or two—not much more—and his or her job is to learn the rest of the skills, so form and voice can be given to any character who comes along. One beginning writer will have an ear for dialogue, another is mellifluously lyrical. So it goes for description, humor, voice, and so on. Every writer can track his or her progression from leaning on the crutch of one skill until a new one was acquired. My first stories were all about setting, and then came stories that were pure action, and then I got point-of-view-happy for a while. And then comes the day—often in an MFA program, sometimes in an old folks' home—when all the skills have to be put together into organic storytelling. The key to learning is maintaining a repository of humility, and it is for posturing against this that I most fault the myths of being an artist. Telling artists-to-be to seek the mystery of writing, rather than the knowledge of it, dooms them to being baffled and unable when they find it.

The great criticism of the MFA workshop is that in discussing any story, a committee will seek the consensus of a middle opinion, thus rounding off any highly original or risk-taking elements, leaving a capable but safe piece of art. Group-think is a genuine danger in workshops, especially when short stories are under consideration. Novels are somewhat different. Though a writer can be a little dictatorial in terms of imposing a will upon a short story, novels are political entities. By political I mean that competing concerns are subject to negotiation and compromise. If, for instance, an author wants to add some extra access to a character's thoughts in a given chapter, the writer will gain a thoughtful, contemplative feel that invites the reader closer to the character. That extra internal narrative, however, is going to come at the expense of pacing, which will then alter the tone, which will then change the mood, and so on. Novels are so complex and interdependent that, like the dialectic of a workshop, every suggested action has to be weighed against many outcomes, some unintended and unforeseen. In that way, a central part of the process of writing a novel is a conversation about the process.

Which brings me to the notion of collaboration. My wife is a novelist, and beyond reading each other's work editorially, we discuss our novels all the time. While writing my last novel, I asked her to help me with an element, and for several days, she roamed through my nearly completed book, typing here and there. A friend recently described making a change in her almost finished book as skipping a rock across the pond: The rock touches water only four or five times, though each one sends rings of concentric circles reverberating outward. So my wife skipped a rock through my book, and it was the better for it. Partly based on that, we decided to collaborate on a project that lasted nearly a year. The work was both wholly thrilling and often maddening. I don't know if what we wrote will ever be published, but I feel as if I did my best work under the influence of a peer, and I'm twice the writer for having done it. Here are a couple things I learned:

The mysterious charge of creating a character-driven narrative was no less hypnotic, though our ability to capture it on the page was doubled. We simply had twice the creative abilities. My wife has a strong sense of voice. I'm good at details. My dialogue is suggestive; hers is smart and sassy. The simple truth is we were able to say and convey twice as much. When I was at a loss, she had a solution, and vice versa. When we both had solutions, we debated. When my precious lines and jeweled descriptions got tossed, it hurt. Sometimes it was simple necessity: We had two good lines and one had to go. Other times, I saw she was approaching a scene differently, striking a different note than I would have or revealing a different facet of character. Those were humbling and valuable looks at another writer's process. Very rarely is one author allowed to enter another's creative space, but once there, you realize the range of ways to evoke character is far greater than you knew.

Usually, the only option for understanding a writer's intentions is to interpret the published work. But when you collaborate, you can ask her as she types.

Commitment became an important aspect of the work, and soon the story was more important than its authors. With ownership less an issue, the focus moved away from us and toward the characters. One result is the fact that we rarely lost control of the narrative, by which I mean we tended not to go off on tangents that suited an authorial fancy at the expense of the characters' progression. Writer's block seemed like less of an issue as we inspired each other and fed off one another's ideas, though we did lose productive days to debate and sometimes argument.

Finally, the conversation about the novel became one of my favorite aspects of the collaboration. Wittgenstein said to measure a thing is to change it. I think that's why humans rarely take stock of their own lives and instead evaluate art. Collaboration somehow made it feel as if we were managing to do both. Leaving no narrative move unquestioned, we made decisions focused on how we could reveal character on as many different levels as possible. The challenge was to demystify the act of writing without demystifying its inspiration. So, like jurists, we sought the truth of our characters' experiences by arraigning their perceptions before the bar of human behavior. I know that sounds like a tall order. It was, and it didn't always work, but if I was to set an ideal model for writing, with the best possible intentions, it would have been this one.

I wish I had been asked to collaborate on just one story for a workshop back in my MFA program. I would have hated it, of course, because it would have meant that I'd have to question all my instincts, that I'd have to get off the crutch of my limited skills, and that I'd have to write a true character for once, a fictitious person who wasn't a disguised version of myself. I would have had to ask, *out loud*, questions like: *What is this story about, what is this scene trying to show*, and *what's at the heart of this character?* And I'd have had to listen to another writer answer. For once it would have been about writing and not about "being a writer."

I'm not suggesting that there should be two names on every book, and I'm sure that, years from now, young writers will still turn to the Bukowskis and Kerouacs for models of how to tell stories that matter. It would be nice to think there was another model, though, one that could inspire a *pair* of young, edgy writers to walk along lonely railroad tracks, kicking rocks and running dialogue back and forth for the story they were writing. Or better yet: a husband and wife team in Nikes, debating about how to close a novel chapter as one folds laundry and the other changes a diaper.

AS WE MEAN TO GO ON

Kelley Eskridge and Nicola Griffith

I don't know how to begin this damn thing, I say. She grins and answers, *Honey, don't faff about. Just tell the story.*

Eight words might not seem like much to run with, but they are all I need, coming from the one who knows my work as well as she knows my body, and who for seventeen years has touched both with grace, with skill, with good intent, with passionate curiosity, with fierce intelligence, with love. After more than six thousand days of living, writing, and talking about it all, I can unpack those eight words automatically; and over a third glass of iced tea I've written this in place of the highfalutin designed-to-impress opening I had. I find this more clear and honest, much as I find myself after seventeen years with her. It's what we do: We make each other better.

The English say, *Start as you mean to go on*, so perhaps it's luck we met at a writing workshop. People warned me these workshops were rough: If I showed weakness of words, of confidence, of self, the other students would bring out the long knives and leave me collecting the leftovers of myself and my precious work in a bucket. But for me, the chance to spend six weeks in the company of students and professionals was like the scene in C. S. Lewis's *The Magician's Nephew*, where the boy Digory stands in front of the bell and the plaque that says "Make your choice, Adventurous Stranger/Strike the bell and bide the danger/Or wonder, till it drives you mad/What would have followed if you had." I've typed all that from memory because it burned into my adolescent brain the first time I read it, so many years ago, when I understood that I would be faced with such choices in my life: that I would have to draw back, or reach out and grab. That's what the workshop felt like. So I quit my job and got a loan and drove from Georgia to Michigan with a left ankle sprained blood-black, bandaged rigid so I could work the clutch pedal with my heel. I was scared witless: of debt, of writing, of not writing. Of those knives. Of finding myself too fucked up to create work that connects rather than distances, and having to go back home with a withered dream, a longed-for identity popped like a balloon.

And then came Nicola. The first time I saw her, in the hallway of the un-air-conditioned dorm, close and hot as a greenhouse, I opened my mouth to say, *How was your trip?* as if we were already each other's friend, lover, partner, joint explorer. I knew in our first three sentences that she would be the best writer there; that I would help her be better; that all my assumptions about how my life would unfurl were wrong; and that I would someday be the writer I yearned to be, because she wouldn't have it any other way.

Sometimes people think it couldn't have been that sudden, that this is just a story we tell. And it is—the first story of us—but it also happened, and is happening still.

• • •

Books—the ones Kelley and I had read, the ones we wanted to write—drew us to the place where we would meet, and made it possible for us to understand each other when we got there. We were born only nine days apart, but also eight thousand miles, on different continents and to different cultures. Our meeting and life together should have been one long cultural car crash, but though there are times when our common language puzzles us extremely, books have formed for us a parallel universe, a world where we learned the same things at the same time from the same characters, though sometimes with distinctly different flavours.

I remember that verse from *The Magician's Nephew*. Vaguely. What stuck in my mind wasn't Digory's moment of choice, but what happened next: The awakening of Jadis, the great and terrible Queen of Charn, in all her six-foot-tall, bare-armed, knife-wielding glory. She immediately became both an eroticised image—like the eponymous magician, part of me sat up straight and thought, ". . . dem fine woman . . . spirited gel"—and a facet of my self-identity. Even today I find bare arms and a desire to take over the world a reasonable response to some situations. And I like knives.

By the time we met, we had both read the quintessentially English C. S. Lewis and the resolutely American Jack London.

We had both read *Lord of the Rings* and internalised it to such
an extent that even from the first day we met, we could quote
it wryly ("It isn't natural, and trouble will come of it!") and understand a variety of meanings, heartfelt and ironic, wistful
and smug, depending on context. We were connected by story;
we came together in that space where character and plot illuminate and influence each other, much as Kelley and I do.

I have fallen in love with Kelley many times—watching her
eat fried chicken with her hands, watching her cry at some
sentimental film, the first moment I saw her limping down
the corridor on crutches in 98-degree heat—but the third or
fourth time was about a week into the workshop when we
were driving to a bookstore for a reading. Kelley was behind
the wheel of her smart red Toyota SR5. A stoplight was lasting
a long time, and she shifted impatiently and said, *"Jan jan jan,"*
a command and an invocation from Frank Herbert meaning
"Go! Go! Go!" and I had come home. I knew that she, too,
had sat curled up on the floor of her bedroom as a teenager,
reading about St. Alia of the Knife learning to slow her
breathing and move her consciousness through time; she, too,
had paused and tried to move a muscle beside her nose or
imagined fighting an automaton stark naked in the moonlight.
In that moment I knew so much about her it was like swallowing the world.

• • •

So how could we not be together? We make story, it makes
us. Like the Worm Ouroboros, swallowing bits of ourselves,

bringing it all back up again. I've always disliked the pictures that show the Worm lying still, tail in mouth, looking vaguely pissed: I prefer to imagine it giving itself a push and rolling exuberantly out of frame. Hooping it up. Off to eat ice cream or go dancing, and tell a good story when it comes home.

It's a human thing to tell stories about how we've become ourselves, to put experience into an ongoing context, so that *here's what happened* becomes *here is who I am*. That's what Nicola and I did when we met. Then we spent a year apart, she in England and I in Georgia, courting by mail. We always make a point of telling people this was before e-mail, so the listener understands it was a serious business, involving much hand-cramping—twelve months and a quarter million words of everyday details, philosophical musings, personal history, dreams, hopes, fears.

Seventeen years later, our lives are webbed, hyperlinked by shared experience, woven into an ongoing conversation of our selves and the two great bindings between us: our love and our work.

"What's it like living with another writer?" people ask. That's a large question. Inside it, some people pack their need for our life to be the stuff of their dreams, storybook-perfect, magic instead of sweat. Others are looking for confirmation that one of us is the Real Writer and the other is Mrs. Real Writer. It's a basic cultural assumption: Someone leads, someone follows; one shines, the other smiles bravely and makes tea. And there's the occasional truly nasty questioner who can't quite hide the hope that writing and love are two horses fighting in harness, pulling in opposite directions, that our work is the slow bullet in the brain of our relationship. "Don't you ever worry that she'll be more successful? I mean . . . " Yes, sunshine, we know what you mean. Fuck you.

I know, I know: It's a fair question, if fairly asked. But that negative baseline enrages me, the default assumption that people aren't capable of living joyfully with ambiguity. What a stupid story that would be. As with all life-altering moments— love, sex, dying, failure, success—the more interesting question is "How do you do it?"

For one thing, we talk. A lot. Elephants don't loom long in our living room: We can't afford to tiptoe around the hard things, because there are too many of them. We talked through the publication of her first three novels, when I was struggling to get a hundred words a week on paper, and felt left behind and frightened to my core. We talked through the short fiction contest we both entered where I won the $11,000 first prize, and she didn't place. We've articulated our agreement that we are each the Real Writer (we feel about writing space the way we feel about everything we own: It's 100 percent hers and 100 percent mine, none of that 50/50 nonsense. Why would we settle for half the space?). She's won a dozen national and international writing awards. I've been shortlisted for a half dozen and never won. *Publisher's Weekly* loves her work and hates mine, but my first novel was a *New York Times* Notable Book. And so on. The truth is, few people would find any meaningful comparison in our careers, or our work, if we didn't rub up against each other in daily life. Proximity and its cousin, influence, turn us from purely individual writers into something else. We map a jointly traveled internal landscape. We have different process and voice, similar definitions of good writing, sometimes-overlapping concerns, and a root system of shared influences.

And we have an identical determination to write stories that touch people, transport them, bring them closer to themselves. So what we do, besides talk, is help each other make that happen.

• • •

The single most important thing we do is tell each other the truth, because writers can't always be trusted to do that for themselves.

Writing is a rush. It's blindingly, incurably addictive. I will do almost anything to dive and swim in that gushing word stream. When the sentences purl forth, when I can do no wordly wrong, it's like being god, or the moment in sex when you step from the rolling, hungry hills onto the vast plain of orgasm, knowing that nothing can stop you now.

So I turn on my music, and I start writing, and I'm lost—Oh, I think, *that phrase is so sharp it'll take their fingers off*—and then I start wriggling uncomfortably in my chair: *Yes, but would that character really do that? Oh, yep, it's all very cool and exciting, but, really, would she do that?*

And like all addicts, I lie to myself, just to ride the high a little longer. *Yes, yes,* I say, *it's fine, don't worry, just keep going. You can make it look right later.* And I can. Like all expert writers, I can spin enough gorgeous sentences and narrative drive to paper over any crack and make the story look good. The crack will still be there, though; on some level, the story won't be true.

True fiction rings pure and clear when you flick it, like a crystal wine glass. If it's flawed, it doesn't matter how good it looks, it doesn't matter whether the prose gleams or the metaphors are as perfect as circles: When you flick it you get nothing but a dull buzz.

Fiction writers churn out flawed story all the time. We lie to ourselves about the essential viability of the work, and then fake it with consummate skill. These cracked works might look good, they might win awards or go on to best-sellerdom, but they are still broken.

So Kelley flicks the novel or the story and tells me what she hears. Most of the time, what I give her rings true but could be improved: word choice, metaphor system, character motivation, sentence structure, pacing, and so on. She tells me so. Naturally, I hate that; there are times when I could cheerfully throw her in a tree chipper.

When we were first living together, and I was writing *Ammonite*, my first novel, I was so grumpy about her comments that she would leave the marked-up manuscript on the dining table and flee to work. For the next nine hours I'd swear, kick furniture, and walk five times around the lake venting my spleen at squirrels and frogs and dragonflies, so that by the time she got home, I could say, *You know, you might be right about that part, with the thing. This nifty little sentence, though, I don't understand why you don't think that works.* And then we would talk.

The normal, everyday way that we work together has remained essentially unchanged: We gird our loins, take a breath, and say, *Ummm, it's not quite there yet. Needs a bit of polishing.* Seventeen years of practice have made us better at it.

The comment-to-acceptance curve is much shorter, and sometimes we can go through six iterations on the same manuscript without me hurting the furniture.

Every now and again, though, we have to deliver seriously bad news. We have to tell each other that something is broken.

I told Kelley, once, that the novella she had slaved over was irretrievable: The characters, the premise, the plot were all wrong, and nothing would do but to throw it away. I felt like a monster, as though I had told a new mother she should throw her baby back into the hospital pool and try again. Every time Kelley hands me something new, I wonder, just for a moment, if I'll have the courage to do that again if I must.

Twice, Kelley has done the same thing for me, once with a story, once with a novella. The story was of no real consequence: I saw almost immediately that she was right. I was a bit miffed, but these things happen. I shrugged, stuck it in a drawer, and forgot about it. With the novella, I nearly didn't listen.

It was a very personal piece—about a woman who is diagnosed with multiple sclerosis—and I thought it was both brave and beautifully written. (I always think that about a newly finished work: My baby really *is* a genius.) I handed it to Kelley, beaming. She read it, looked troubled, and said, *I don't think this works.* I frowned. I stayed calm. I asked why: Was it the imagery? The character? *No, no,* she said, *they were fine.* What, then? She frowned and said she needed to think about that. Two days later, she was still thinking: She was sorry, but she couldn't pinpoint the flaw; I'd papered it over so well she couldn't find it, but it was there. The story didn't ring quite true.

At this point we'd been living together seven years. I trusted her. So I took the novella apart looking for the flaw. I held it up to all the bright critical lights I could bring to bear; I hefted it, emotionally, and found it pleasing; I ran through the phrases in my mind, and I couldn't find anything wrong. Not a thing. I agonized: I believed Kelley, but I couldn't find the flaw. Maybe she was wrong. So I sent it to a small magazine and by return mail got a contract, for what at the time was a princely sum, and a letter of fulsome praise. I signed the contract and cashed the check. But I felt uneasy, as I usually do when I rationalize. That unease grew, and grew, and grew, until one day about three months after I'd sold it, I took the novella out of a drawer, and flicked it one more time, and listened, and heard a sickening buzz. I still didn't know what was wrong with it, but clearly something was, so I returned the money and told the editor I was very sorry, but I was pulling the story. *Why?* he said. *I don't know,* I said, *but it's not right.*

Now, of course, I know what the problem is—but it's taken me years to figure it out. And one day I'll rewrite the piece, only it won't be a novella, and everything in it will be different.

So Kelley and I try to keep each other honest. We don't always manage it with equanimity. But we keep telling each other what we think, and we keep listening because we know and trust each other and each other's work.

It also helps that we're extremely aware of the differences in that work. We often joke that our worldview and our writing—process and product—are diametrically opposed. I write from the outside in, and Kelley writes from the inside out. My focus tends to be physical: The character moves through its environment, and what she notices about that environment becomes a reflection of her internal journey. My metaphors are geophysical, environmental, physiological. Kelley's focus, on the other hand, is emotional. Her characters have nuanced, delineated interior lives. Her metaphors are cultural and pop-cultural and interpersonal.

It's been fascinating in the last few years to see the beginnings of a crossover in our work. Kelley's is becoming more environmental, mine more interior. I don't think we've lost anything by this; I prefer to believe we've enriched and deepened our skill set. If I'm lying to myself, I'm sure Kelley will tell me. Sigh.

• • •

I will always tell you, darlin', the same way I will always be honest about the work, although there are days when I'd rather jump in the tree chipper all by myself.

This persistent, sometimes ruthless clarity has become part of our bedrock. It's not just in service of each other, although that's a good enough reason: It's in service of the work itself, and our shared belief that writing can, and should, be true rather than clever. Glam prose is like salt-and-vinegar chips: Easy to eat, hard to stop, and tastes so good that it's only later people realize all you've really fed them is a giant potato. And yet, I yearn to be a rock star of writing, I really do, and my constant challenge is to strut, to wail, to put my guts on parade, to grab the reader's heart and head and hips, to create meaning that makes them move not just because it is a pretty noise. Pretty doesn't make my meal. Perhaps it would if I had not met and married as I have, but it's too late now: Someone who loves my love of rhythm and riff, and understands how it can slide out of tune, sits across the table from me every day and holds me to my own center. That's the crux of it: Nicola doesn't help me make my work more like what *she* thinks it should be, but what *I* think it should be. She helps me reach for my vision of my writing, as she helps me reach for my vision of my self.

So here we are in this marriage where love and work are inextricably connected. Behind it, as with all marriage, is our constant effort to define the lines between self and other in professional as well as personal terms, and our trust that these lines will hold no matter how far into each other we step: boundaries that are not necessarily barriers, permeable but not passive. We're strong people. We could push each other toward our own image, but it's better that we don't: It might be more comfortable to have identical notions of how words best weave together, but it's better that we don't. Our differences allow us to give to each other without losing ourselves.

All our influences come together in the stories we tell. It's an exciting time to be a writer, with so much fodder for story available, only a mouse click away from the hopes, dreams, fears, and experiences of others. People are webbed together physically and psychically in ways whose consequences we're only beginning to understand, with such potential for resonance and connection. Story is no longer the preserve of the few: Anyone can make a blog, a Web site, a movie and the soundtrack to go with it. This can be troublesome for writers: Public dissemination of text, formerly the great divide between the amateur and the professional, is now possible even for folks who couldn't find a felicitous phrase with both hands. As a result, the writer is becoming less separate from the writing: The edges of public and private identity are blurring. As we have more access to the world, it has more access to us.

I think this frightens some writers: That which was a barrier is now only a boundary, more permeable than is perhaps
comfortable. But this narrowing of the gap between writers
and readers is a joy for people like me and Nicola, who are accustomed to the tension of self and other with regard to our
work, and who welcome the chance to connect with readers
in ways that enhance their experience of our text. Which is
the key: As much as I want to be a rock star, I'm resisting the
impulse toward the Cult of Me. My connections with readers
are about the work: how it is to read, to write, to become part
of each other's story for a little while.

Nicola and I manage these connections primarily through
our Web sites. (Why doesn't every writer have a Web site? I
don't know. It's a mystery.) The heart of these sites is not the
information about us, or our work: It's the forums we've set
up to interact with readers. People who submit questions or
comments to Ask Nicola (hers) or Virtual Pint (mine) will
get a response from us, and sometimes from other readers.
What started for each of us as a random Q&A is becoming a
conversation, as questions build on one another and ideas
cross-connect.

I love Virtual Pint. I knew when I began that many readers
who enjoyed my work would delight in safe access to me (it's
less vulnerable than raising one's hand in a bookstore). I didn't
expect to find the same joy in it that I do in conversation over
beer and a Philly cheese steak sandwich in my neighborhood
pub. But perhaps it shouldn't have been such a surprise: After
all, it's just another way to connect. To share story.

· · ·

But what story? We are complex creatures; the stories we build and tell are overlapping, contradictory, and always under construction. The story I tell in a novel isn't the same story I tell on my Web site, which isn't the same story I share in a deep conversation with a friend. The telling and listening change us, which changes our story, which changes us: on and on, as endlessly as a fractal.

I think of the text of a novel as a blueprint and the novelist as architect and builder. I might specify where the walls and windows go, the height of the ceilings; I'll decide on the elevation and orientation, but the readers provide their own experience and tastes and furniture. They paint the walls and move the doors and put in light fixtures, add the hideous horsehair sofa and hang wishy-washy watercolors over the fireplace. One person moves into my text and turns it into a chintzy cottage; for another it becomes a minimalist temple. Every reader inhabits a different novel.

One of the things I love about a truly great novel is that if it is built well, I can read it over and over: As the years pass, as I change, it does, too. I discover in it new truths.

Our experience changes our truth. In that sense, the influence Kelley and I exert over each other and our work is enormous. We bring each other bits of the world the other might otherwise ignore. She surfs blogs and tells me what's going on in the pop culture world; I devour *The Economist* and explain the (to me) hilarious English sniping. She gives me the latest mashup to listen to; I bring her gosh-wow science news about developments in quantum teleportation or ambient information delivery. I drag her off to watch wide-screen historical epics where people whack each other's heads off with swords;

she persuades me of the value of seeing Serious Films full of Anguished People.

We share with each other, we change each other, and then every day we have to decide how much of ourselves we share with the rest of the world. Most novelists wrestle with the question of what to put in or leave out of our fiction. It's a paradox: We want to tell people our truth, but we're terrified of being seen and known. Here's another paradox: I believe firmly that it's a mistake for a reader to assume she knows the details of a writer's life from reading her work, but I also believe that if you have read all of my novels you have an essential grasp of how I regard the world. The details are fictional, but the essence shines through. I can't hide it: Most of me doesn't want to. Trying to hide is probably the major contributing factor to bad fiction. (Impatience and lack of talent are the other two.)

Fiction isn't the only forum to consider. I started Ask Nicola on my Web site a few years ago and now have hundreds of thousands of words addressing questions ranging from academic and philosophic esoterica to "I think my granddaughter is a lesbian. What should I do?" I have to learn how to answer using only my own internal compass and long conversations with Kelley—because there are no guidebooks about this stuff; it's too new. How honest should one be? How guarded? What do my readers deserve to know? What do I want to tell them?

The Kelley and Nicola you meet via VP and AN are not quite the same Kelley and Nicola you might meet at a party, but if you'd read even a handful of ANs and VPs, you'd easily connect the person with her text. I'm sure that shocks no one. What shocks me—despite experiencing the same thing over the last seventeen years while living with Kelley—is the extent to which answering questions truthfully about my work influences that work. For example, someone asked a year ago about the role of music in *Stay* and *The Blue Place* and the stance from which the narrator thinks about music: I didn't know. I said so. But I knew that was the easy way out. I promised the reader I would think about it, and I did, while brushing my teeth, or chopping vegetables, which led to discussions with the reader (a composer), and to several scenes in my new novel where we learn more of the narrator's past, her relationship with her mother and her attitude to the world, through her interaction with two different pieces of music. I wouldn't know all those things about my character if it hadn't been for that initial question and the thought triggered by trying to answer it truthfully.

What this reader did with a question, Kelley and I do for each other every day. We reflect and illuminate, we ask the questions of each other and expect deep, considered answers. Asking and answering changes everything.

Meeting Kelley changed everything. I felt it, the first time I saw her. There she was, limping down that corridor—I could barely breathe it was so hot; the air was like warm potato soup—and I saw her and thought, *Oh.* Every single cell in my body lined up like iron filings and pointed at her. She is my magnet. And she is my book. I read her over and over.

HER DARK SILENT
COWBOY NO MORE

Neal Pollack

I used to invite people I didn't know to send me e-mails. Sometimes I'd receive forty or more a day. They were something I craved. I'd published a book that had achieved "cult" status. Cults never end well, but you don't realize that when you're at the center of one, even a small one that mostly exists on the Internet. To me, the e-mails meant I was sticking in the collective consciousness of a subset of people unified only by the fact that they'd read my silly book, or knew my silly name. I enjoyed the mild electric charge that came from knowing I had a small amount of power over a few people's minds. The e-mails watered that little seed of megalomania that lay in my gut, waiting for nourishment.

One night, I received an e-mail from a young man that went, in its entirety: "Neal Pollack is a dick dick dick dick dick dick dick dick dick licker."

If I were to read those words today, I'd erase the e-mail immediately and return to whatever useful task I'd been pursuing before it appeared, writing or checking my rotisserie baseball statistics or eating lunch. But in those days, I was still pretty drunk with myself. I wrote him back immediately.

"Dear ____," I said. "Thank you very much for the nice e-mail. I appreciate you taking the time to write. However, I'm disappointed that you didn't spend more time explaining yourself. Do you really think I'm a 'dick licker'? If so, why? What does it mean to be a 'dick licker' anyway? I don't understand, so here's what I want you to do: Take that initial sentence and turn it into a story. The story doesn't have to be very long. In fact, I'd prefer if it were rather short. Call the story "Neal Pollack Is a Dick Licker," for all I care. But make it a story. If it's good, or even marginally coherent, I will publish it on my Web site."

About three weeks later, I got a follow-up e-mail from the same young man. This one had a Microsoft Word document attached. To my delight and relief, the attached story was not called "Neal Pollack Is a Dick Licker." Instead, it was a boxing melodrama. My spelling and grammar checkers detected no mistakes. So I sent it to my webmaster and immediately had him put it up on the site. A few months later, I actually read the piece. I'll summarize it for you here:

A boxer named Jerry Rubbo snorts cocaine in a locker room. He talks to his trainer, a pug dog named Hooch, who is fluent in English, French, Chinese, and Esperanto. Hooch informs Jerry that he will be fighting me tonight.

Well, not me, but rather "Neal Pollack," an imaginary boxer who has "had 67 fights and he's never lost, not once. Truly, just one man ever even managed to draw blood, and that's only because he worked part-time as a phlebotomist."

The story continues. Neal Pollack, apparently, also has a Dalmatian named Crazy Willie Spots for his trainer. Jerry enters the ring, where he sees Neal Pollack shooting heroin into his left eye. I quote directly from the story now:

Jerry stepped up onto the apron, which is the matted area just outside the ropes of the ring, as well as an invaluable piece of clothing, most often worn in the kitchen or by hookers dressed up to look like sexy French maids. It was just a matter of minutes before he had made his way onto the inner apron. Pollack, noticing the show, pulled the nail he had hammered into the palm of his hand out of his hand, used it to pick the shards of glass from out between his teeth, and then stepped into the ring himself.

The fight begins. Jerry throws his first punch. Pollack, on major drugs, freaks out because he thinks Jerry's glove is a giant gopher that's going to eat his face. From there, the story grows incoherent. Jerry wins the fight, but as the crowd swarms the ring, he dies of a brain embolism. Pollack is trampled by the crowd and also dies. The author reveals that this legendary fight has led to the banning of drugs from all major sports, "except for archery."

How satisfying that piece was for me at the time. I felt like I'd encouraged another young writer to do his best. It was, to my mind, a brilliant piece of fan fiction.

• • •

My first book, *The Neal Pollack Anthology of American Literature*, was comprised of first-person satirical essays, loosely connected, about "Neal Pollack," the "Greatest Living American Writer," contemporary of Norman Mailer and Gore Vidal, acclaimed novelist and literary journalist, sexual adventurer and world traveler. The character bears my name, but other than that, no closer resemblance to my real self than to a talking pig. He's a sort of blank slate for parodic buffoonery. The *Anthology* was the first volume published by McSweeneys Books, which at the time had a substantial Web cult of its own. After a few people had read the book, I began to receive fan fiction.

The first came from a guy in Seattle who imagined a world in which he attended a reading of mine and actually managed to pick up a woman there because of his association with me. It was a nice sentiment, so I published the piece on my site. Then I got an e-mail from an angry fellow, appropriately named Chris Kilgore, who said, essentially, that he wanted to kick my ass because I didn't deserve the "fame" I was receiving. I wrote him back saying, essentially, that instead of wanting to kick my ass, he should write a story about how he wants to kick my ass. If it was reasonably good, I told him, I'd publish it. Then he'd be doubly blessed.

A few weeks later, I received "I Will Beat Neal Pollack to a Bloody Pulp." In the story, a nameless narrator takes a charter plane to Los Angeles, but it crash-lands in Kansas instead. There waits "Neal Pollack" in a wheat field. He pokes out the narrator's left eye and then proceeds to grind him bloody into the dirt, but not kill him. As the story ends, the narrator shouts out, "I'm alive, Pollack!" Then, "Somewhere within me there was a searing heat that Pollack's Aura hadn't smothered."

I published his story. He left me alone. And the fan fiction kept on coming.

• • •

Since I'm in the mood for pretentious generalizations, let me say that you can tell a lot about a society by the stories it has in common. Our culture is so fragmented, our population so enclosed in its little shells of community, that the only real unifying thread, story-wise, comes from television, and, to a lesser extent, movies. Television characters live inside our minds as though they're actual people. In fact, we know more about them then we do about most people in our physical lives. It shouldn't be surprising, then, that people piss away millions of words every year writing fan fiction.

Most fan fiction is terrible. Much of it is incomprehensible. Some of it is insane. The briefest Google search reveals extensive fan fiction sites for the usual dorky television suspects: *Xena: Warrior Princess, Buffy the Vampire Slayer, The X-Files, Babylon 5, Stargate SG-1, Doctor Who*, and any superhero you can imagine. There are also fan fiction sites for *The Nanny, Nash Bridges, Remington Steele*, and *Party of Five*, among many other completely forgettable items of popular culture.

To illustrate this point, I bring you a scene from "21 Jump Street—Fallen Angels," by a Ms. Sarah Lubin, which probably makes sense to only the truly dedicated fan:

> Tom walked down an alley without a flashlight and without his partner, Doug Penhall. He blew a piece of brown hair out of his face. A crunching of a can echoed in the alleyway. Tom thought it was Harry. "Harry?" asked Tom as he walked farther into the alleyway. He wished he had brought a flashlight. The moon was supposed to be a full one, except clouds were covering it. A gunshot echoed. Tom spun around, to be greeted by a rather large hand. Before he could scream out, the hand grabbed him and covered his mouth. Another hand grabbed the gun and pressed it against Tom's face. "Hanson?" yelled Capt. Fuller. "Are you okay?"

The most popular form of fan fiction is "slash," stories that posit gay relationships between pop culture protagonists. The Ur-document of slash is a *Star Trek* fanzine, begun long before the feverish subreality of the Internet, which documents the ongoing love affair between Captain Kirk and Spock. For reasons that cannot and will not be investigated here, women write the majority of slash fiction. Take, for example, the story "MacGyver: All Work and No Play," by Meg Bruck. Here's a telling sentence: "They kissed as passionately as they so often fought, while Murdoc pumped Mac to breathless completion. MacGyver came with a groan and melted into his chair in a boneless and satiated heap." Oh, yeah. Oh, baby.

Obviously, these television, movie, and comic book characters have profound, even mythic, significance to the practitioners of fan fiction. Otherwise, why would the writers
produce stories, some of which run into the tens of thousands
of words in multiple chapters, especially considering that their
work will be seen by, at the most, only a few dozen people
with a similar kink?

These writers aren't professionals, or if they are, they're
hiding behind several thick layers of pseudonym. But they
have characters in their heads, even if they're stock characters
created by professional TV drudges sitting in windowless
rooms in Hollywood. It's a long way down the myth slide from
Beowulf to *Sabrina, the Teenage Witch*. Still, fan fiction authors
are perpetuating their characters, extending their universe,
and they're damn serious. I found one anonymous writer on
the Web who discussed her craft as intelligently as anyone
who contributes to the *New York Times*' "Writers on Writing
Column," and with far less pretension:

> Nearly 100% of my fiction was written *before* I tried to
> define what I would define as "good." I did use spell-
> check and I usually rely on a beta reader. That's about it.
> The truth is: I have some bedrock beliefs about writing,
> and about fanfic. Chief among these is that talent makes
> a difference. And that very few fanfic authors have any
> real talent for writing. On the other hand, attention to
> detail will take even an only marginally talented author
> a long way. Characterization, exposition, description—
> be careful with these and you can turn out some darned
> good stories.

I took this advice to heart as I started writing my first novel, *Never Mind the Pollacks*, a 256-page fictitious history of rock music starring a character named Neal Pollack. That fan fiction philosophy certainly applied to what I was doing more than, say, E. M. Forester's *Aspects of the Novel*. My self-absorption was at its all-time height. I was now writing fan fiction about myself.

Let me tell you how far I descended into the madness. In March 2002, I announced a "Neal Pollack fan fiction" contest on my Web site. The three winners, I said, would receive a hardback copy of the *Anthology*, signed by me. I knew that anyone who would enter such a contest would more than likely already own a copy of my book. I had that figured into the cost.

I received forty-five submissions. Some of them were not, technically, fan fiction, since they didn't feature a character named Neal Pollack. A few were just disgusting. But most were quite good. I put up thirty fan fiction pieces on my Web site. One was a James Bond–style thriller that took place in the Pyrenees. Another was called "An Excerpt from the Journal I Kept Whilst Neal Pollack and I Were Stranded in the Distant Past, on a Floating Island Made of Dinosaur Manure, Out of Smokes and Withdrawing Slightly." There was a story featuring Neal Pollack as a character in *The Lord of the Rings*, and a script of "Pollack's" appearance at the worst poetry open mike in history. There were also several slash fictions, including one cleverly called "My Love Affair with Neal Pollack."

I also received something called "Talk of Important Things on a Summer Day," by a guy from Brooklyn I'd met once at a reading. He told me I was the only person to ever publish his fiction, which made me feel good. Fan fiction might actually have some relevance, I thought. It's a nice place for a young writer to start, a jumping-off point for the imagination. Why, I was inspiring people while maintaining my very own literary cargo cult! What writer could ask for more?

Along came "Her Dark Silent Cowboy," written by a woman named Shannon Peach, which she assured me was not her stripper name. The main character was Trixie, a waitress in an all-night truck stop diner. . . . "She is not a skinny little thing," Ms. Peach wrote,

> but juicy; ripe for the fucking, her Uncle Hal used to say with a fond glimmer in his eye. She accessorizes with fishnet tights that reach mid-thigh and a pair of sturdy boots. She wears no panties, just in case. Just in case of what, exactly? Just in case a real cowboy ever walks in, a Neal Pollack, a road warrior with spray-painted on jeans and a package like a summer sausage.

·Later, came this sentence, which, in retrospect, was the highlight of that period of my literary life: "Neal Pollack undulates his hips so slowly she thinks she might go mad."

• • •

HarperCollins published *Never Mind the Pollacks* in the fall of 2003. The book certainly has its moments, though the audience of people who can really get an Iggy Pop joke is pretty small. Despite a lot of hype, much of it generated by me, the novel didn't do all that well. Reviews were mixed, and I do mean that there were some positive reviews. However, the *New York Times* ran a hit job that described me as "an ordinary humor dork, yet another 35-ish, doughy white man with a goatee and thinning hair." A personal slam like that doesn't belong in the country's most widely read book review, but I have to say that the guy got everything right, except the part about the goatee. Enough of this "Neal Pollack" crap already, I thought.

I got really depressed, which tends to happen after five years of relentless self-aggrandizement ends and you're left with nothing but an empty husk of what you once wanted to be. Then one morning I got an e-mail from someone I didn't know. "Surprise," it said. And there was a link.

An Internet humor site had, with the collusion of some of the many friends I'd made online, decided to throw me a "roast," without my knowledge or my permission. Over the course of a week, dozens of Web sites were going to roast me, and I was powerless to prevent them. On the one hand, it was flattering that these kids, and they were mostly kids, thought enough of me to fling crap at me for a week. On the other hand, roasts can go terribly wrong, and we all know that the Internet can go terribly wrong. I knew I was in trouble when the illustration for the roast's home page was a photograph of my face with the head of an erect penis grafted on top.

Most of the roast entries were harmless. My friend Dennis wrote a funny fake news story headlined "Neal Pollack Captured by U.S. Forces." Another friend published some fake e-mail correspondence between us with the title "Where'd That Balding Jackass Pollack Go, Anyway?" There was a fake series of anti-Pollack insults by the deceased Henny Young-man. These were along the lines of stuff I'd seen before, maybe even a little bit better, and I enjoyed reading them.

The lead essay of the roast, written by someone I'd never met and had barely corresponded with, called me, ironically, "The Most Important Artist of Our Time." I think the follow-ing excerpt speaks louder than any slash fiction could:

> Where real artists reinvent themselves, Pollack simply paints his tired little gimmick a new color and pushes it back out there, foolishly confident that nobody will rec-ognize it as the same old schtick in a different hat. In-deed, Real-Deal Neal has somehow consistently parlayed his far-reaching Genuine Suckiness into the self-aware Just-Pretend Suckiness of Pretend Pollack, by masquerad-ing as a (terrible) pompous, intrepid journalist, as a (terri-ble) snarky, social-political-media pundit/critic/blogger, as a (terrible) rock 'n' roll warhorse, and as a (terrible) performance artist. In the end, he's a jack-of-no-trades: talentless, unoriginal, yet successful by way of his own incompetence.

Reading this tore at my gut, particularly since, again, there was some truth to what the guy was saying. I'd opened myself up to this treatment because I'd made myself so accessible on the Internet, and also by behaving like a braying ass for nearly half a decade. Still, upon rereading the essay, I think the guy who wrote it meant well.

Not so, I believe, a piece by someone I *did* know a bit, who wrote a scathingly critical essay that repeatedly referred to me as a "Jew bastard," called me far less talented than any of the other writers I occasionally consorted with, and apologized to my then one-year-old son for the fact that he (the writer) was going to have to kick my ass.

I e-mailed the guy and humorlessly ordered him to immediately remove all mention of my son from the piece. Then I e-mailed a friend of mine, another writer, who the "roast" writer claimed I compared to unfavorably, and then my friend wrote the roaster an e-mail, tearing him a new one, and the resulting melodrama was as exhausting as it sounds.

The roaster ceased and desisted. He took the piece off his site, but not before asking my friend and me if he could publish our exchange, which he said had been "revealing." We said no. Then he published a long apologia on his site, and yet another obscure Internet cockfight pecked its way toward a pointlessly melodramatic conclusion.

These were, as my fan fiction period goes, the last wasted guests left at a particularly decadent and self-absorbed party. They'd grown incoherent and somewhat cruel. I sat on the couch, broke, with a semifailed novel to my name, and unsure about how I was going to support my kid for the rest of his life. The next day, I published a somewhat histrionic good-bye to my "fans" on my Web site, then immediately retracted it, and then said good-bye again. I canceled the e-mail address to which people had been writing me for years. No random citizens could ever contact me again, with the exception of the organizers of MoveOn.org, who always seem to find their target market. I was thirty-four years old. If I was going to write for a living, I was going to have to write about something other than myself, or at least my fake self. I decided that I could bring the "Pollack" character back from time to time in well-paying venues, but I would relieve myself of the absurd burden of carrying around an eponymous persona. That crock of shit had really started to stink.

A few months later, someone pointed me toward the Web site of my cruelest roaster. In a secret place, he'd published e-mails people had sent him about our little controversy. He was very "conflicted" about the decision, he said. Some of the responses defended me as an unwitting victim. Other people had said I'd received exactly what I deserved. Both sentiments were probably true. But my favorite response went like this:

> Now that I have looked at all the inanity that was written for this completely inane project in the first place, and wasted this much time even just THINKING about Neal Pollack and any of the other dumb people who bothered to waste their time thinking and WRITING about Neal Pollack, I am officially through. And if you insist on being part of any more of this completely juvenile, inane, idiotic "community" of people who have nothing better to do with their time and no better ideas than to spend their time making fun of Neal Pollack, then I, for one, don't want to hear about it.

Me either, dude.
Me either.

YOUR OWN PERSONAL SATAN

Glen David Gold

I published my first piece of paid writing in March 1994, in the *East Bay Express*, a free weekly distributed across Berkeley and Oakland. I spent much of that week going from café to café, waiting for someone to pick up the paper and begin reading my article so I could come up to them and tell them I wrote it. Typing that, I cringe. Nonetheless, I recall my dedication on my lunch hour, on my way home from work, on the little walks I took after dinner that just happened to amble past the Coffee Mill, Café Roma, Sufficient Grounds. I was relentless.

I'd spent six months working on that article, eight thousand words on my internship at Suicide Prevention. My byline's appearance was the culmination of a dream I'd had since grade school. And, goddamn it, I wanted to see someone who was ignoring his or her latte in favor of my piece. "Yeah, I wrote that," I imagined saying, with a squint into the noonday sun, and a tilt of my chin into the wind, as if I led safaris, as if this encounter was no big deal.

After four or five fruitless days, time was running out. I saw a woman in her late sixties reading the *Express* in Café Trieste. In fact, she was halfway through my article. I couldn't believe my luck.

I stalked her. I pretended to look at the paintings on the wall. I went to the phone and gazed back at her. She wasn't looking up. She didn't touch her scone. Instead, she folded the page back and kept reading. This was awesome.

Finally, I approached her. When I said, "Hey there," she looked up.

"You liking the story?"

"Yes, I am," she said. She pursed her lips, gazing past me as if she had something to add.

But I just plowed on. "Great, because I wrote it."

"I'm hoping this article can explain to me why my son killed himself."

Pow.

In my fantasies of surprising readers with my presence, this was never the response. What did I say back to her? I must have mumbled something acknowledging her loss, but I would like to replace whatever I said, from the beginning, from the approach, with a slow backward tiptoe away, hands extended, occasionally whispering a sincere "I'm sorry . . . I'm sorry."

To find a reader engaged in your work is incredibly rare, up there with finding a unicorn laying his head in a virgin's lap. Stripped of pretence, my ambling up to her and grinning, dusting my nails and blowing on them, actually meant, "I am insecure and looking for reassurance and hoping to perform this bait-and-switch: If you loved my words, surely you'll love me, here I am now, love me! Have I mentioned I am so trapped in my desires that I can't even conceive that your reading is a private act? LOVE ME!!!"

This was a blunt-force lesson that should have ended for me a fantasy that I think writers have had as long as there have been readers: the desire to be a fly on the wall, what Paul Bowles calls "the invisible spectator," as your work is being discussed. Seeing that woman's pain ended, forever and ever, my desire to know what people think of my work as they're reading.

Sort of.

Ladies and Gentlemen, my name is Glen G and I google myself.

If, as Depeche Mode promises, we all have our own personal Jesus, then Google is my own personal Satan. It pains me to explain Google, as it's like trying to rationally describe what fishnet stockings are: They're just clothes! Why all the fuss? Google is a search engine whose effectiveness at ferreting out online information is sublime and terrifying. It is the site that chews up all other sites and digests them, an enzymatic action leaving a fibrous residue that reflects only the subject you're searching for. And I look for Glen David Gold.

The results come back in fiendish little packs of ten, the name of each site crowning strips of text lifted from that page, often rendered broken and opaque. Google works like an ocean storm, scattering upon my own particular beach all the pretty seashells that reflect my name. For instance, it reports back to me that the *City Insider* of Glen Clove, Maine, features a fortune cookie summary: "Glen David Gold finds meaning of holiday in poor man's soup." This is a bizarre tease, for, alas, the page itself is no longer found, the meaning of that soup long gone, Google simply savoring the aftertaste.

Google is mighty, like Uranus, and, like Uranus, eats its own, sitting on a lonely, towering throne made of zeros and ones that, in macroscope, are actually the crushed and mangled egos of every poor soul on earth who types his own name in the "search" box. When you look into Google, Google looks into you, and not to get Miltonic on your ass here, but like the moon shining at the whim of the sun, the reflected glory you find is actually the unremarkable glow of the second-best, not what you're actually looking for, a spark of human love.

Which might be a bit overdramatic. When considering my own vices, I tend to reach for the rafters, if only to beat my head against them.

A bit of genetics here. My father has worked with computers since the 1950s. We had a computer terminal in the house in 1970, a bulky plastic podium whose every key made a resounding ca-chunk sound, like crushing pistachios, whose protorenaissance of a brain required punchtape that cast off extremely satisfying confetti into a translucent side pouch fantastically attractive to six-year-olds in search of things that went well with the wind. There was a phone umbilicus, which connected this little beast to its mother downtown, a mighty DEC 10 mainframe. My father spent hours every day hunched over it, typing away in BASIC or FORTRAN, and being separated from it caused him enough anxiety so that our housekeeper called it his mistress.

I believe I learned from my father that it wasn't wrong to spend sunny afternoons and Saturday nights immobile in front of a computer. The dishonest and lazy side of me would like to drop the blame for my Internet addiction at my father's feet, but I can't quite hold my head up to that. It's entirely my fault.

In 2001, I wrote a novel called *Carter Beats the Devil*. If (as of today) you put my name into Google and hit "search," you will come up with the first 10 of a claimed 6,950 pages that mention me. On the right-hand side of the screen, you'll see "sponsored links," which make intriguingly related promises. At eBay, for instance, you'll find "Low Priced Glen David Gold! Huge Selection!" Which I have to admit makes me feel rather cheap (and mildly excited). And eBay has in fact an astonishing heap of my novel, in aggregate a tower perhaps thirty stories tall, with frighteningly low opening bids. The next sponsored link, Reunion.com, is more personal and less about turning me, Glen David Gold, into a commodity. "Reunite with David Glen," it promises, which honestly tugs at my heart in a sappy kind of way until I remember that my name is Glen David.

To follow the results on Google takes a kind of obsessive-compulsiveness matched only by chain-smoking insomniac laboratory gibbons who feed slot machines for cocaine pellets. After Google automatically removes all similar sites, there are 730 web pages that mention me. I have looked at each and every one of them, all the way from the Duran Duran fan site (a fan recommended *Carter* to Simon LeBon) to the Suicide Girls Web site (a patron of the Suicide Girls has *Carter* as a favorite read) to sites memorializing Philo T. Farnsworth (who appears in *Carter*) to the alt.sexuality.spanking newsgroup (it was suggested that a scene I wrote in which a pirate burned the back of a pretty girl's hand with a cigarette "capture[s] perfectly a certain type of intense emotional connection that can happen—if we're very very lucky—as we do what it is that we do.").

Ah, the intense emotional connection. Is that dangling carrot why I do this spinning on my wheel? There is the obvious desire to be paid attention to, but I have to admit that straightforward reviews of my novel, even if they're generous, aren't what catch my attention. I am charmed by the tangents, the way people all bring their own perceptions to the party (I hadn't intended to make a sub/dom statement using a pretty girl and a pirate as my mouthpiece, but hey, cool!). I like how, as with the best of all grace, we touch people in unexpected ways. But that's not all of it—there's some underlying anxiety that sends me back to the well.

I notice this most when Google pops up with a phantom sentence in its display, random poetry dragged out of hyperspace and slammed still between the glass sheets of a microscope slide. One of Google's findings has the bizarre heading "Re: paleonet Freshwater Coccoliths," which caught my attention (there are no coccoliths, freshwater or otherwise, in *Carter*). And below it, I saw the terrible-looking incomplete phrase, " . . . Carter as woefully inadequate," and I clicked, almost shaking with rage ("Who the hell finds my *Carter* to be woefully inadequate?") to find that the phrase was my own, part of a quotation I'd used in my novel and now part of the signature for the Chief Consultant, Industrial Nannoplankton Gower Street Laboratory in the UK. I was relieved.

And perhaps that's one key to this obsession: the sudden emotional shock and then return to normal. It's like watching a horror movie. Perhaps that's it, entirely.

Or not.

Recently, I was standing around with a group of friends, all writers, and I cheerfully announced I was going to write an article about googling yourself.

There was a cough, a lonely sound, a tumbleweed rolling across the floor.

"Looking people up on Google?" one guy finally asked.

"No, yourself."

"I only look up other people," he declared, adding with a certain triumph over me, "It's handy when you're dating." There was much agreement, and the conversation turned elsewhere. It closed the metaphor: Googling yourself is like masturbation. Only not sanctioned. You are allowed the *shame* but there has of yet been no Jocelyn Elders, no Joani Blank, to tell you it's OK to do it.

I'm not sure I'm the fool to rush in with that particular message. Unlike masturbation, which has a genuine end point and—when done adequately—some satisfaction, self-googling just goes until it stops. Even though my father was actually getting work on the computer done rather than whatever the hell you'd call my obsession, I think I know how he felt when being called to dinner or to bed, or when confronted the next morning and asked if he'd been at the computer all night: There is a suspicion that just after the next mountain, awaiting you is the finale of truth, a completed task, and you can finally log off once you've laid it bare.

A few months ago, Google reported that my name appeared on a Web site I'd never heard of. It was called fivesandwiches .com. Fivesandwiches.com's heading said it was a site dedicated to reviews of audio and print books. The text below, as often happens, was noncommittal. There was no way to tell what the site had said about me. So I clicked on it.

My cursor turns into a small yin-yang sign when something is downloading. I suppose I chose it to remind me of patience. You know, the way you do.

Fivesandwiches.com took its time. First the frame showed up, with a logo in the upper-right-hand corner: five cartoony, triangular wedges, speared with toothpicks, boasting olives, greens, and layers of meat, iconic 1950s man-about-town sorts of sandwiches, the kind of sandwiches Rock Hudson would have toyed with in *The Pajama Game*.

The site ranked novels on a scale of one sandwich to five sandwiches, five being the best, one being the worst. But the information specific to me was slow, oh so slow, to download. The yin-yang sign spun as all the side text and links appeared, along with invitations to save *Angel*, the television show; updates to *Doctor Who* newsaramas; interminable links to sponsors that sucked up processing time; and then finally there was my author photo, with a link next to it: Show me the books by Glen David Gold. Nowhere was it mentioned exactly how many sandwiches I'd been given.

So I clicked again on the link to my work, and once again my cursor arrow went Eastern philosophy on me, and while I pondered the ironic collision of Taoism and unbridled egotistical impatience, I wondered: Was my novel just three sandwiches, perhaps? Four? I'm sure I was a five-sandwich book,

and any fewer would be an insult. What if the bastard gave me
only one sandwich? What did he know anyway? What books
did he like? Bad books, I was sure of it. I remember Lou Reed
complaining on *Take No Prisoners*, "How would you feel if you
spent a year and a half on an album and some jerk from the *Village Voice* gave you a B+?" and I felt an even more savage kind
of formula: five years on a novel and a judgment of only *one*
sandwich? How dare he judge me! And judge me via a measure
of sandwiches? Why sandwiches? Who the fuck would use
sandwiches as a critical yardstick? Surely anyone whose judgment was so impaired as to rely on sandwich-as-paradigm
couldn't be trusted to render a proper opinion on literature.

And why *five*? If anything, my novel deserved to be off the
friggin' scale. I wanted the first-ever rank of *six* sandwiches. No,
a hundred sandwiches, a hundred million billion sandwiches.
Goddamn it, then, the dream of raw, unconditional love: I
wanted *Google* sandwiches.

Finally, my review appeared on the screen. I had five sandwiches! It took a moment to recognize it, and to retreat from
feeling disappointed that I hadn't gone off the charts. Five
sandwiches was solidly on top. Which was great. There they
were, lined up, bounteous and wholesome and friendly. Clearly,
the webmaster was of uncommon thread and perceptive eye.
Sandwiches were cool. And amusing, if you thought about it.
He followed his own drummer, and I loved him. The review
below it was one sentence long, "Glen David Gold presumably
spent his life working towards this excellent book," which was
a wonderful thing to read, and then it concluded, "and I doubt
he will have another such novel in him."

Pow.

There was nothing else. No explanation or follow-up. There is no real way to pick up a Web site, turn it over, and shake it, but I more-or-less did the equivalent with my mouse, following every single link, wondering why the hell he thought I was finished, until I realized that was that. Judgment rendered.

I looked at my watch. I'd spent twenty minutes on this site, coveting imaginary sandwiches. The review was so perfectly written, such a sucker punch of a single sentence, the thrill of "excellent," followed by the train tracks falling five hundred feet, "I doubt he will have another such novel," that I felt shame at having pursued it. And it dawned on me: All it would take is a lifetime of working mornings scrolling through sites like this, and he'd be absolutely *right*.

Not that it can simply be hand-in-glove like this, but ever since fivesandwiches.com, I haven't looked myself up on Google. Oh, it's one day at a time, and if there were meetings for people like me, I'd go to them, but then I'd probably spend hours online looking up everyone else in the group.

But no, now I'm free, and so I can spend my long afternoons awash in the spirit of true creativity, playing epic, consecutive hands of computer solitaire.

MARGINALIA AND OTHER CRIMES

Tara Bray Smith

I have misplaced my pen. Or I don't reach to get it anymore. I don't know why. I used to always read with a pen in my hand, as if the author and I were in a conversation. *Ha!* I wrote. *Wow, Gosh, No!* In Homer's *Odyssey* I scribbled: "Being tall is important," and "Doesn't everyone just want to be safe and sound?" I "analyzed": *Fresh green breast = Daisy* and *Odysseus = The Middle Way.* No one ever admonished me not to write in my books, so I never considered it wrong. Library books, my own books, the books of friends. (Let him who always returns his borrowed books cast the first stone.) Seeing the words issue from my hand, in a fine script, purple Pilot Precise Rolling Ball V5 Extra Fine, no dull black ballpoint for me, made me understand the books I was reading. So I wrote to learn. Or I wrote to be private. The book was my bower. I wandered off. Page 68 of *Pride and Prejudice:* a list of imaginary names for

unborn children. Isabel, Minden, Ezekiel. Minden is the name
of a town in Nebraska I passed once. Not the town, just the
name, on a sign, next to a field. Isabel was a great-aunt. Did I
not see how silly these names would seem to me in ten years?
Ezekiel. How embarrassing. But who cares? I never minded
the random scribblings of other readers; found them interesting, in fact. It is a truth universally acknowledged that people
write the darnedest things in the margins of their books.

Someone told me a long time ago to put my pen to someone else's paper. Who was it? Mrs. R—— from high school,
who sent her charges into rapture one day around the holidays, 1986, when instead of instructing us, she read Truman
Capote's "A Christmas Memory" aloud in a reedy, great-aunt
voice. Any teacher who favors reading aloud to sentence dia-
gramming is my kind of teacher. And it was Mrs. R——'s notion that one needed to have a conversation with the author,
with oneself, by writing.

Here's Sylvie, in turquoise hi-liter, in D. H. Lawrence's
Complete Short Stories, Volume 2 (I found her at the Strand):

> Dear Sasha
>   I'm writing today
>   this sort of short
>   letter, to tell you
>   that I hate you.
>   'cause you're a
>   bitch. My big bitch.
>   You're a goddammit,
>   a little twerp, ugly

a jerk, a mental
defective, a twit
a scatterbrain
a whore, a dike.

SyLvie

A *goddammit!* Exuberantly crass, of unclear sexual prefer-
ence, SyLvie likes "The Odour of Chrysanthemums" through
page ten or so, underlining here and there in a desultory hand.
She favors dramatic words (so like her, Sylvie) and hot phrases:
slunk, red coals, mumbled, rapturously. Then nothing.

Sylvie interrupts my reading, her intrusions thicken "Chrysanthemums'" delicate nose. But I like Sylvie. I like her guts.
Hell, I like the fact that she reads at all! To analyze the moral-
ity of whether or not she should be there, in my book, seems
beside the point. Certain bookworms eat books. Eat them,
swear in them, spill things on them. There are still books in
the Philadelphia Free Library's children's section that have
bits of pages—corners, mostly, but also the occasional edge—
missing because my friend Elizabeth ate them. Tore them off
and popped them in her mouth. Most notably: *The Five Little
Peppers and How They Grew; Rose in Bloom,* by Louisa May
Alcott; and perhaps the *Shoes* books—*Dancing Shoes, Ballet
Shoes, Theater Shoes.* Her favorites were the oldest books, because the pages were salty.

Reading, for me, is like this: consumptive, pleasing, calm-
ing, as much as edifying. It's how I feel after a good dinner.
That's why I do it so often: It feels wonderful. The book is
mine and I insert myself into it, cover it entire, eat my way

through every last slash and dot. That's something you can do with a book, unlike television or movies or the Internet. You can eat it, or mark it, like a dog does a hydrant. (Though Web marginalia software is being developed, it is still not widely used. The closest the Web gets to true marginalia is the posting area of blogs, and even this is more composed than your typical "Huh?" written in the margin of a paperback. Unless you conceive that the entire Web is a kind of marginalia, written on the Ur-text of us. But back to my subject.)

There is this marking aspect—book as object—then there is something else. Reading as conversation, except all at once, with the reader given the benefit of someone's completed thought sitting there in front of you, ready to be digested. And here, the meal metaphor again. Perhaps this is why books are so compelling. They leave room for us. They offer themselves to us, entire, to be taken at our whim. To lift our eyes from the page, to go to the bathroom without having to press pause, to put our book aside for years, and not miss a single scene.

Of course there are certain books one must not write in (I know that!). Library books, for example, though I have cheated. There is something so self-absorbed, downright priggish about "Marginalia and other crimes," as the Cambridge University Libraries call the act of note taking, philosophizing, arguing, personal organizing, what-have-you in library books (www.lib.cam.ac.uk/marginalia). And yet I insert one query (I can't stop myself): Isn't self-absorption—and its opposite, complete mind-meld with another—what reading can be at its highest? And really, on the scale of things, is it so bad? In a Gutenberg Bible, yes. But in *Wine for Dummies?* Yes, of course, if the book's not yours. Though I would have to include my own dirty doings under the heading "Case 4: Marginalia, single author many books," or perhaps "Coloured marginalia," or even the mysteriously titled "?," I prefer the innocent carelessness of "Case 3: Damage by animals, small humans and birds."

So thank the household gods for the pocket-sized paperback, where you can write whatever you want to. Those little wafers of pleasure, issued by the gazillions starting in the 1920s and 1930s, reaching their modest zenith in the 1960s, when television was still in swaddling clothes. Illustrated by Edward Gorey, Milton Glaser, Andy Warhol, now a dollar a dozen. Worth so little they are put in basement laundry rooms for the taking, which is how I got *What Maisie Knew* and *Deliverance* and *Lord Jim* and Patti Page's *Once upon a Dream*, in which "Lovely Patti shares her intimate secrets of popularity, diet, beauty, love and marriage." These books are extra. They accumulate on stoops, their pages humid and curled, F R E E hovering above them like a plea. They are what poor men sell on the Avenue of the Americas and are humbly beautiful like all good, free things: sun, air, water, grass, stars, love. They are to be written in, bent, thrown into bags. They should function as stories and diaries and confessionals. (Inside SyLvie's Lawrence: "Jesus had a twin. He knew nothing about him.") They should accumulate all manner of stains: coffee, dirt, newsprint, ink, water, pigeon droppings, food. Sand and pressed leaves should fall from their pages.

Sing to me of Signet Classics. Penguins and Puffins and Peregrines and Plumes. Bantams ("Read more" in the back always tempting me to send ten cents in) and Meridians and

Fawcett Crests and Doubleday Anchors. Vintage and its worried little sun, Pockets, Popular Library Fictions, Mentor Editions, Pyramids, and Heinemann's African Writers Series, Founding Editor Chinua Achebe. Sing to me of Comp IV, Am. Lit., Freshman Comp., Brit. Lit., Edith Hamilton's *Mythology*, *A Separate Peace*, the purple cover of the *Color Purple*. Sing USED SAVES (George Washington Bookstore Textbooks), $4.95 reduced to a buck, down to a quarter, finally nothing. Sing to me of muted spines in red, yellow, green, taupe, manila, manila, manila. Sing of that blunt little typeface Times Roman, and those otherwise unloved nineteenth-century portraits that would not have lives unless put on the covers of Oxford Classics. Sing to me of dog-ears,

*

!

?

]

Yes!

Doodles and grocery lists and phone numbers I do not recognize anymore, and boys I once loved. "Woman as object," "Man v. Nature," "Wow!," "Gosh!," "SELFISH BITCH," "No!!," "Careless people," "Blah blah," and the eyes of Dr. T. J. Eckleburg. Esteemed eds. Alvin Kernan, E. M. Butler, J. P. Hardy, L. J. Swingle—where are thee now?

Those lists. Those lists that made me feel inadequate. READ THESE OTHER VINTAGE TITLES. I was twenty-four. I put checkmarks next to every book I had read and there were only one or two on each page. *Lolita*, *Dubliners*, *Light in August*, *Ragtime*.

And yet I did not write in all of them, and even now will not as often pick up a pen. Why did I not write in the margins of *One Hundred Years of Solitude*? Or *Where I'm Calling From*? Or *Père Goriot*? (Michele Peter's copy has only one mark. On page 82, Madame de Beauséant's speech against love: "I've read very extensively in the book of society, but there were apparently still a few pages I didn't know. Now I know them all.") Ed Quaintance's copy of the 1957 New Directions paperback edition of *Siddhartha*, by Hermann Hesse, has a black-and-white Buddha on its cover. A mean boy with blue eyes gave the book to me in high school. I thought it meant he liked me. He did not. There are a few dog-ears. They trot out after a few dozen pages.

I didn't write in these books because there was no pen around, most likely. But then, there are writers that speak to us more or less directly. The Greeks, for example: "No one wants to speak the truth," I announce to a blameless Herald in *Agamemnon*. But poor Ibsen, whom I quite like, nothing, de Tocqueville's *Democracy in America*, nothing. James's *The Bostonians* is empty, so is *Romeo and Juliet*.

Yet *Franny and Zooey* has its requisite haphazard black ball-point underlining:

He wasn't Epic*tet*us.

"—you don't just despise what they represent—you despise them."

Do we grow out of responding to our books like this? Or do our books become more imposing as we age, less like friends, more like mountains to climb? I read J. M. Coetzee's *Disgrace* without a pen; though I loved it so much I had to hold my breath and look up several times while I was reading it. Yet

not once did I get out a pen. It was just in my bag, at my feet.
All I had to do was reach over.

Billy Collins, from "Marginalia," on reading *Catcher in the
Rye*:

> —*I cannot tell you*
> *how vastly my loneliness was deepened,*
> *how poignant and amplified the world before me seemed,*
> *when I found on one page*
> *A few greasy looking smears*
> *and next to them, written in soft pencil—*
> *by a beautiful girl, I could tell,*
> *whom I would never meet—*
> *"Pardon the egg salad stains, but I'm in love."*

Competitors to the written word have matured. Television
is not so stupid anymore, is it? And I hardly watch it. I don't
have one. Not because I detest it; in fact, I love television too
much, the way it fills in the spaces. It's brighter, and in some
sense, easier, all the while becoming more complex, more interactive. TiVo as fire hydrant. My untidy stacks of Doubleday
Anchors and Mentor Editions have a hard time competing,
no matter who illustrated them.

Still I wanted to read today. It's August. The weather this
summer has been fine. I have a new-old paperback—Coetzee's
Foe, Penguin ("—is that the secret meaning of the word story,
do you think: a storing-place of memories?"). It has been lent
to me. Its previous owner did not like it much; or at least, I
imagine so, as it has not been written in. But even here you

can see Mr. Coetzee gathering steam. "Bright future!" I would write in the margins.

And here is where the book, and especially my humble cheap-or-free book, is still best. It is not tethered by electric cords or determined by central programming or mediated by actors or accessible by remote or trapped in a rectangle of glass. It is not too fancy or rare to be brought to the riverside. It is a tangible, physical thing, something to be held, a perfect, common thing that can be spilled on and tossed into a bag and even lost and *Oh no, I'll have to get another one.* Pardon the egg salad stains, but I am in love.

I will bring a pen. I will lie in the grass. I will look at the river occasionally, and then I will look back at the words on the page.

SECURITY

Benjamin Nugent

For a few months I contributed to a gossip column that accorded Paris Hilton the level of coverage *Prevention* accords cancer. Like the columnists in Evelyn Waugh's *Vile Bodies*, my colleagues and I were parasites on a parasitic aristocracy, and it was sort of empowering. Our job, I learned, was to disclose the secrets of people who never seemed to work, for readers who considered themselves overworked and undervalued. We slaked a thirst for schadenfreude and a thirst for escape. We made Paris Hilton a character people needed.

The novelists and short story writers of my generation offer the same release: They put the reader on intimate terms with characters who don't think that often about work. I find this striking because jobs have been the dominating issue of my adult life. Jobs have affected how I relate to my family, where I live, and whom I'm in love with, and jobs have consumed the vast majority of my waking hours. I can't imagine writing a novel in which jobs are not a central concern. Would I be a better writer if I had the money to study writing at Columbia or African drums in Vermont, or to lock myself in an apartment with a manuscript and a portrait of Solzhenitsyn? Few young writers have Hilton's resources to play with (I mean this in a strictly monetary sense), but the Northeast is full of nonstarving novelists-to-be who do nothing terribly lucrative. If I were one of them, would I write mostly about extraprofessional matters, as admirable writers roughly my age—Jonathan Safran Foer, Zadie Smith, and Nell Freudenberger—have done? Foer's *Everything Is Illuminated* is about an American Jew named Jonathan Safran Foer exploring the fate of Jews in the Ukraine, and a Ukrainian translator with a distinctive grasp of English. Cross-cultural relationships are also the most prominent recurring theme in Freudenberger's story collection *Lucky Girls*. Moving between East and West is the single greatest theme in Zadie Smith's first novel, *White Teeth*. It's not that jobs aren't described well; they're just not the center of attention and identity.

There is a small subgenre of fiction in the George Saunders vein that explores the metaphorical and comical possibilities of the protagonist's surreal work life—often at a nightmarish amusement park or roadside attraction that serves as a microcosm of the world outside. But that's not the same as a realistic portrait of jobs a lot of people actually have, like banking, like waiting tables. I don't know of any young voice offering realistic portraits of contemporary American lives defined by normal, time-consuming, soul-altering occupations. None of this constitutes a failure on the part of the writers I've mentioned; it's simply a choice of focus, or a respectable compulsion toward a particular set of subjects.

I'm apt to wonder if I'd write less about work, and perhaps be a better writer for it, if I had a trust fund. Wouldn't an allowance give me more time to write, and make it more natural to create warm protagonists whose lives are not defined by their jobs? I had a trust fund at one point, and its effect upon my writing—perhaps even more so the effect of its departure upon my writing—was considerable.

England's Labour government won reelection in 1966, when my father was in college. Shortly thereafter, the way my father tells it, an alumnus who lived nearby came to eat at my father's club, to which he'd once belonged, and found himself in a crowd that shared his Tory sympathies. My father was a Labour booster, and a vocal one.

"Aw, come on," he said, "give the socialists a chance." The old conservative and the young liberal were thus introduced and became friends.

When I was in preschool this alumnus gave my father a job running his charitable foundation. My family visited him on his estate outside Boston every couple of months. My memories of it are precious: paintings by major impressionists on the walls, ships in glass cases, a ballroom, a green, rolling field speckled with white geese behind a big brick house. As I got older and my father moved on to new jobs, we visited less; when I was in junior high, I accompanied my father on our first visit in years. The alumnus was feeble now. With death so near, he said things he used to keep to himself. As he ate lunch at the head of his long dining-room table, a tall window shedding golden light over his wild gray hair, he spoke with unusual tenderness about a man my father knew.

"I used to descend upon a village in China," he said, "and a thousand little Chinese boys would soon be calling my name."

"Bringing joy to those who otherwise would not have had it," said my father. "That has been your life."

When he died shortly thereafter, it turned out he'd left a fund for my sister and myself, to pay for our education—more precisely, a fund for the children of my father.

My father informed us of this development in a five-minute family meeting, the longest discussion about it we've ever had. There might have been a whiff of Dickensian fairy tale about the windfall—a benefactor descends and frees a brother and sister from ordinary toil, or in this case having to apply for financial aid for college—but my father made it clear we were not to think of the investments that way. He was terse and vague about the money and the rules that governed it, making clear that the news should prevent us only from worrying about college tuition. He forbade us to talk about it to anyone. My sister and I have talked about it obsessively ever since, and in an exceedingly vulgar manner. So many questions arose: Just how posh did this make us? Was it OK to start drinking a lot of scotch? This store called Brooks Brothers came up occasionally in movies—could we maybe go?

For despite my father's wishes we'd been infected with a sense of security, exacerbated when my father married my first stepmother, a magazine editor who lived in Manhattan, drove a red BMW, liked Jil Sander, and, having grown up with a stepmother herself, knew to treat us like friends rather than offspring. When I left for college and my sister for boarding school, my stepmother's prosperous father paid for both, presumably reducing the strain on the trust fund. He volunteered to pay for my second year, too. I began to tally how much cash would be waiting for my sister and I when we graduated.

The idea of inheriting money was especially appealing because we'd grown up mostly with our mother, who never had any money. There were a lot of unpleasant boys like myself raised in Massachusetts college towns by single mothers in grad school living on child support and part-time jobs, and we were terrorized by kids from the neat subdivisions that rose between the orchards. They hated our hand-me-down clothes, our mumbling hippie locutions, our incompetence at sports, and our generic sneakers. How could people dressed that way put on airs of knowingness, of sanctimony, the way we did? What kind of secret did we think we had on them? We couldn't even shave right—what was our *problem*?

In accordance with my reputation in high school, I tried to write the way teens with bohemian aspirations all over America do—exactly like Allen Ginsberg. When my stepmother rolled onto the scene, the *Howl* impulse gradually gave way to a more genteel—more cosmopolitan, I believed—world-weariness and humor and restraint. Soon I'd be part of a bigger, warmer, more free-spending world. What was there to get so embattled about?

The decline of this personal Belle Epoque began about two years later. My stepmother divorced my father, which ended her father's funding of my education, weekends at her familial hideaways, and Miu Miu dresses for my sister. My father started dating a woman who wanted children. By the time I graduated from college at twenty-one, I had a second stepmother who was pregnant with a child who would require schooling from Upper West Side preschool onward. Another child followed thirteen months later. The gorgeous baby boys were just as much the children of my father as my sister and I, and the fund was explicitly created for all children of my father, rather than just my sister and me, the extant children at the time of its establishment, so there was no discussion; after graduation I was going to get nothing. When I finished college in 1999, my father and stepmother lent me the security deposit for an apartment in a slum in Brooklyn, and that was that. I was trust-fund-less. It was time to put the sweater vests in storage and invent a new, more hardened accent. It was time to find a job.

My first job was with a Hasidic real estate agent, showing apartments to other Brooklyn greenhorns on commission. He stole a commission from me and threw me out.

My father knew the parks commissioner. To my dismay his people gave me a job in a rec center in Brownsville, Brooklyn, finding permanent full-time jobs for people enrolled in its welfare-to-work program. I slouched around the office with an air of profound martyrdom. The clients were mostly middle-aged single mothers of asthmatic children. I had just turned twenty-two. My title was Employment Expert.

The cant of the boomtime worked against me; when I found a potential secretarial job for one strong-willed young woman, she turned from her toddlers, who had discovered my filing system, and told me to find her work at a foundation. "That's fulfilling," she said.

Usually, I would send the clients out to chase a lead I'd uncovered for them in Manhattan. They would shrug and mutter something about how it was too far away from where their children went to school. I would insist they should try to get it anyway, and they would trudge to the subway in pairs. They did not return employed. At one point during one of the morning pep talks I gave, a Jamaican woman lifted her head and screamed.

Roused from the ghoulish stupor of self-pity in which I lived, I asked her if she was OK.

"It is just so pointless," she said. Then she went back to looking up herbal remedies on the Internet.

She was right, of course. When I gave up trying to help anybody, because I'd scored my first magazine job at *Life* and given two weeks' notice, the clients and I started to have amiable conversations about music, TV, and the Civil War. They explained they were never going to work very far from their homes because of the asthma attacks their children were always having. A daughter's school would call to say she was on a stretcher, and there would be nothing for it but drop the bar code scanner and escort her to the hospital. They'd had jobs before, and the regularity of medical emergencies had gotten them fired. Or they hadn't had jobs before, but they'd heard from their friends that such an outcome was to be expected. They were holding out for a theoretical receptionist position that would allow them to escape to an East Brooklyn school district whenever they needed. They were biding their time attending my workshops and spiking trash in the parks wearing green vests with the parks department's leaf insignia on the back. This was what they did to keep their benefits.

I had lucked into a job as an arts reporter at *Time* just after *LIFE* shut down and started to write about people who thought about money and work a lot. I didn't realize that this was kind of fifteen years ago. Some of the most famous American novels published when I was in grade school, across a wide spectrum of literary prestige, and including books by young writers—*White Noise, The Bonfire of the Vanities, Bright Lights Big City, American Psycho*—hit their highest notes rifling through the protagonist's office. DeLillo had his department of Hitler Studies, McInerney his coke-fueled fact-checking procedures, Wolfe his hungover gossip writer, Ellis his demented financier. Michael Lewis got rich when he ditched his Wall Street job to satirize Wall Street in *Liar's Poker*. Then, if novels are a guide to such matters, we slacked off a bit and devoted more time to family and ancestors.

What happened? It's a familiar argument that our field is increasingly cloistered and professionalized, that writers are concentrated in dewy glades where neither cars nor televisions disrupt their communication with God. According to the *Chronicle of Higher Education*, fifty American colleges started new creative writing programs between 1996 and 2002; between 1992 and 2002, according to the nonprofit organization Associated Writing Programs, the number of graduate writing programs nearly doubled. No doubt a direct plunge from college to MFA program to professorship could deprive a writer of contact with the corporate and business worlds in which more typical careers unfold.

But I wonder if the more important factor is that it's gotten harder to be the kind of nine-to-fiver who writes before and after work, to be William Carlos Williams scribbling poems on prescription slips between patients. For the statistics on work are clear: Jobs take a bigger bite out of our lives than they used to. In a survey cited in the *New York Times* in the fall of 2004, 62 percent of respondents said their workload had increased in the past six months alone. A front-page *Times* story from July showed that Europeans curse the sky and follow us into a more Spartan work-to-leisure ratio. It's a trend that works to deprive us of the poem by the doctor about her patients, the novel by the judge about the defendant. Would Wallace Stevens have written *The Emperor of Ice Cream* if his day at the insurance company had been thirteen hours long?

You can't blame writers for turning to academia. But the result is that as we work more and more, young writers write about work less and less, distinguishing themselves by exploring different ethnic and national cultures, which is something people do in English departments. We do not read much about the varied forms of employment that create such wide gaps between perspectives, such different everyday lives.

And still the public, despite its Hilton fixation, displays an appetite for stories about work. Look at television (if you're reading this book it's possible that you would benefit from watching more television). *The Apprentice* is pornography for people who daydream behind a counter at Wendy's about stabbing the salad bar guy in the back in order to make shift manager. All over Los Angeles, proud TV writers sell their Miatas because of shrinking demand for the sitcoms about families they used to write. The reality shows that marched over the sitcoms offer a kind of sublimated workplace in which the object is winning a Darwinian struggle for money.

Look at commercial fiction. *The Nanny Diaries* and *The Devil Wears Prada* not only sold well among people steeped in the lore of Upper East Side parenting and the offices of *Vogue;* they were national publishing phenomena, presumably at least in part because they describe the experience of being a relatively poor woman working for comically awful rich women. They trade in humor about posh drudgery and the relationships between bosses and peons. Allison Pearson's novel *I Don't Know How She Does It,* another success, revolves around the problem of how to be both an accomplished professional and an attentive mother.

Of course, all three of those titles draw quite directly from their authors' experiences; the fuss over the first two started because they seemed to be tell-alls clothed as fiction. It's a different task to imagine what other people's jobs are like, in much the way writers my age have so adeptly put themselves in other people's ethnogeographic perspectives. I'd like a writer of my generation to perform the task the parks department set me (and in which I so spectacularly failed): understanding work lives and work-related aspirations that are exotic to middle-class creative people. What's it like to be a twenty-seven-year-old Republican lawyer working seventy-hour weeks in San Diego? Or a twenty-six-year-old restaurant manager in Dallas who works two jobs to support two children? A security guard at the Woolworth building who moonlights tending bar off Wall Street?

Let's face it; my generation will probably be defined partially by its military response to the aggression of radical Islam and aspiring superpowers, but it will also be defined by its economic response—its inglorious pursuit of money. I don't mean class, or the right table at the right restaurant, but money. Money to send your kids to an adequate school, money to retire without all that much pharmaceutical deprivation, money to be able to float for a while should a job disappear, money to pack your family off to a country house if an office building down the block gets blown up, money to stop working so many hours when you're no longer young. Money to buy that elusive, intoxicating sense of security shaping up to be one of the delicacies of our age.

In so many contemporary novels, the ethnic makeup of a family has a real, if not transfiguring, effect on a character's life. (This is not true just of fiction by "ethnics"; Jessica Shattuck's WASP-y heroine in *The Hazards of Good Breeding* feels confined to a small world.) The trajectory of *my* life has been set by the movements of dollars, and not even remotely by the fact that I am half Jewish and half Irish. I write fiction about people who obsess about jobs and money because I can't imagine people who do not. If I succeed, I will capture the repressed panic, the incessant scrambling, and I will become my generation's literary Employment Expert. I could sure use the work.

PART THREE

• • •

THE NOW

DISTRACTIONS

Tom Bissell

All this new technology
will eventually give us new feelings
that will never completely displace the old ones,
leaving everyone feeling quite nervous
and split in two.
　　—DAVID BERMAN, "SELF PORTRAIT AT 28"

Ours is an infantile generation—though I do not intend this as an attack. If you were born in the fourteenth century, you were a part of the Plague Generation whether you liked it or not. Video games, action films, the power ballad—many of us are endlessly distracted by the infantile and, however ironically, love it, consume it, defend it. Comic books were my greatest distraction. This is not exactly a blockbuster confession. With all the people coming out of the comic closet these days, I keep expecting Louis Farrakhan to cop to a secret love of *The Uncanny X-Men* or *The New Mutants* or *The Legion of Superheroes*. Of course, I loved all three, as well as *Swamp Thing* and *The Avengers*. They were My Favorites. Needless to say, I have not kept up. At a certain point, the travails of Kitty Pryde, Sunspot, Dr. Alec Holland, Lightning Lad, and Vision ceased to command my attention. Comics typically attend to a peculiar sort of adolescent alienation. The genius of early Marvel comics, as many have previously noted, was their introduction of profound emotional estrangement into the lives of superheroes. DC comics, until the mid-1970s (when the Green Arrow and Green Lantern, most memorably, found the former's young ward, Speedy, in a grimy men's room with a heroin needle plunged into his arm), had virtually none of this. Yet Peter Parker was a weak, dateless dork who lived with his skeletal aunt, Bruce Banner endured a constant terror of his own emotions, the Fantastic Four were riven by a long-standing love triangle, and the X-Men lived within the oasis of a Westchester County mansion that protected them from the very society they had pledged to safeguard. Anger, frustration, rejection: These heroes felt it, too.

Eventually, however, one grows up. The alienation inherent in donning colored spandex and going head-to-head with Kraven the Hunter ultimately proves less compelling than the alienations one begins to feel around the age of fourteen or fifteen. Having been hopelessly transformed into a reader by comics, I turned to books. Opening *Rabbit, Run* in study hall as a fourteen-year-old high-school freshman, stumbling dumbfoundedly across lines such as "Rabbit goes to his wife and, putting his arms around her, has a vivid experience of her—her tear-hot breath, the blood-tinged whites of her eyes" made me conscious for the first time of a writer's individual voice. Prior to *Rabbit, Run*, I merely read books for their stories. Even Stephen King, whose novels I ripped through one after the other, did not affect me the way Updike affected me because I read King for *what* he wrote about, not *how* he wrote about it. But I felt behind Updike's prose an unfamiliar urgency, a need to communicate some larger, scarier truth than automotive demon possession or the vampire next door, no matter what pains King took to ground such phenomena in the soil of the convincingly mundane. *Rabbit, Run* implanted within me an awareness of what I can only call writerly consciousness.

Updike once told *The Paris Review*, "When I write, I aim in my mind not toward New York but toward a vague spot a little to the east of Kansas. I think of the books on library shelves, without their jackets, years old, and a countryish teenage boy finding them, and having them speak to him." I grew up quite a lot, rather than a little, to the east—and way north—of Kansas, but I was certainly a "countryish" teenage boy, and the *Rabbit, Run* hardcover I read had long shed its dust jacket and was not years but *decades* old. I will not succumb to the narcissism of believing that Updike was foreseeing me, or even anyone like me. I will, however, admit that the first time I read this interview I wrote Updike a fan letter in which I succumbed to the narcissism of telling Updike he was foreseeing me. Enough, though. The book spoke to me, just as he had hoped it would, and by the time I finished *Rabbit, Run* I wanted to read writers, not books. I was getting drunk on the hard stuff of literature, and I read with the reckless greed of a fresh and emboldened addict.

As for my comic books, I said my own good-bye to all that and sold them for a song to a particularly unpleasant eighth-grader named Mike Myers (no relation). Occasionally I am bitter about this, as many of my comics would today be worth good coin. I owned the entire Chris Claremont–John Byrne run on the *X-Men*, for instance, the first fifty issues of *The New Mutants*, Byrne's entire *Fantastic Four* run, the first Alan Moore *Swamp Thing*, and many of Frank Miller's now priceless *Daredevils*. When I am honest with myself, though, I remember that most of these issues were too mugged and scruffy from my constant reading to have been very profitable, as only "mint" and "near-mint" comics are worth much of anything. That said, I can scarcely bear even getting into how one Gus Hookinson, my neighborhood bully, connived his friendship-feigning way into my home in order to pilfer from my collection *The Incredible Hulk* #180 and #181, the first and second appearances of the Wolverine ("The world's first and greatest Canadian superhero!"). At the time of the Hookinson Deception, these comics, which I kept in Mylar bags and never read, were worth forty and eighty dollars, respectively, as Wolverine was, even in the pre–Hugh Jackman era, one of the planet's most popular comic book characters. Today, both issues are worth thousands. I should, alas, point out how I came into *Hulk* #180 and #181. The teenage son of a friend of my mother's drowned in Lake Michigan, and she gave me his collection. When I first came across *Hulk* #180 and #181 in the drowned boy's bedroom I knew perfectly well that they were worth quantitatively more than their twenty-five-cent cover price, but I said nothing. The still heartbroken mother would have given them to me anyway, I am sure, but I believed—I still believe—that my moral failure to inform her of the real worth of her dead son's comics propelled Gus Hookinson into his damnable though fated errand of karma redistribution. Even so—goodbye to all that. However, there exists in my childhood another, defiantly unadult pursuit at similarly distracting loggerheads with the calling of serious literature. I speak of video games, which I am, to my mild alarm, still playing.

Let me say that I do not really believe that anything, other than rank stupidity, is in itself antithetical to literature. But to live a life that values literature above all else requires some stark decisions about what one will and will not devote time to. This question of wasted time is, I believe, of especial importance to writers my age, as we grew up in and now live amid a world filled with an unprecedented number of time-sucking lures. Probably every writer comes of age believing that, at least in terms of distraction, writing is harder for her generation than for all those that came before. Every writer has been correct in that belief. Human culture keeps producing newer and technologically cannier things with which to distract itself. For instance, while writing this essay, I have been playing speed games of computer chess. No doubt Willa Cather and John Cheever had their own distractions from writing, but the ability to swap queens with their typewriters was not one of them.

What chance, then, will future writers have against this onslaught of infernal machines? A good number of older writers and critics have written of their fear that the corpus of literature will turn slowly rigor-mortic as the energy and devotion of the young are consumed by the jumpy pixels of visual entertainment, be they in films or video games. I have some sympathy for this position, for I fear the same thing. But might this not be vanity? We all enjoy believing we are the final keepers of a sacred flame. Only the sturdiest sort of crank would hold that films, as an art form, are inferior to literature anyway. Films demand a different sort of commitment than literature, certainly, and provide a separate kind of pleasure, and though I personally believe that the commitment to and pleasures of literature are of a higher caliber than those of film, I also know I say this as a writer and devoted reader. In other words, I recognize my belief for what it is: chauvinism. Which does not mean I believe it any less. Artists need their convictions, especially those that protect and justify their allegiance to their art. Less chauvinistic is my belief that the written word, the bridge that spans recorded history, is central to human civilization. Moving images are central only to the twentieth century, if that.

As for video games, very few people over the age of forty would recognize them as even a lower form of art. I am always wavering about where I would locate video games along art's fairly forgiving sliding scale. All I know is that, art or no, my enslavement began with a refrigerator-sized stand-up console known as Space Invaders. The Midway game, which first appeared in 1978, four years after I was born, was already regarded as a bit of a relic by the time I discovered it in the opening months of the 1980s (meanwhile Nintendo was still a playing-card manufacturer). I remember the first time I played Space Invaders so vividly because my stepfather had just suffered a massive heart attack and was undergoing emergency bypass surgery in Milwaukee. My mother was relieved that the hotel we were staying in had a modest arcade because it distracted me from the very likely possibility that my new stepfather, to whom my mother had been married for less than a year, might not survive. Thus, sitting on a hard and sticky barstool, my pockets leaden with quarters, a hotel worker in my mother's secret employ watching over me, I played Space Invaders for hours. The Upper Peninsula of Michigan, where I grew up, did not yet have any video games, and during the following months of checkups and tests I returned with my family to Milwaukee several times. I think I believed that only Milwaukee had Space Invaders. To this day, the word *Milwaukee* floods my mind with involuntary images of dive-bombing amoebas and digital bulwarks slowly annihilated by enemy-insect offensives. My mother claims I went into something like clinical withdrawal whenever we left Milwaukee.

I was far from alone in my youthful enchantment. Space Invaders was so popular the world over that Japan suffered an economic crisis due to a serious shortage of 100-yen coins, England held public hearings on the problem of Space Invaders–caused truancy, and the *New England Journal of Medicine* recognized "Space Invader wrist" as a medical condition. The machines were not only affecting children. In 1982, the novelist Martin Amis published a little-known (and, today, impossible to find) work of nonfiction entitled *Invasion of the Space Invaders: An Addict's Guide to Battle Tactics, Big Scores and the Best Machines.* The book's foreword was surreally provided by Steven Spielberg, and the jacket photo showed Amis leaning familiarly against a stand-up Missile Command console. "Now I had played quite a few bar machines in my time," Amis wrote of Space Invaders, "but I knew instantly that this was something different, something special. Cinematic melodrama blazing on the screen, infinite firing capacity, the beautiful responsiveness of the defending turret, the sting and pow of the missiles, the background pulse of the quickening heartbeat, the inexorable descent of the bomb-dumping monsters: my awesome task, to save Earth from destruction!" It is oddly inspiring to read one of my favorite living writers address video games with such rapture—and weirdly dissonant with the Amis who would later write of nuclear weaponry with such brilliant scorn. Amis, more troublingly, went on, "Now, after nearly three years, the passion has not cooled. I don't see much of Space Invaders any more, it's true. . . . These days I fool around with a whole harem of newer, brasher machines. When I get bored with one of them, a younger replacement is always available. . . . The only trouble is, they take up all my time and all my money. And I can't seem to find any girlfriends." Girlfriends, indeed: the anti-video game. I am reminded, here, of the end of a highly pleasant date with a former girlfriend. When the cab pulled up to her apartment, she invited me, unambiguously, inside. I told her, with convincing regret, that I had to work early the next morning. Ten minutes later the cab dropped me off at my friend Jeff's, where we commenced with a Tolstoyan sally of video-game playing that lasted nine hours. When I confessed my lie to Jeff, he said something that still manages to turn my circulatory system arctic: "Would you ever have imagined when you were fourteen that one day you'd be turning down sex to play video games?"

The fact is, if anyone told me at fourteen that when I was thirty I would still be *playing* video games I might not have lived to see fifteen. Much of this self-hatred, though, is theoretical. When I am actually playing video games I do not mind so terribly, since I typically play with friends. When I play alone for any extended period of time, on the other hand, I am by session's end typically ready for a hemlock gimlet. But just as I could not have imagined at fourteen my video-game-playing life as a thirty-year-old, I would have proved as powerless in imagining how amazingly *good* video games were going to get. It happened so quickly! We went from Space Invaders to Frogger to Centipede to Donkey Kong to Tron to Colecovision to Intellivision to the Great Leap Forward of the first Nintendo home system. This is a climactic event in the typical video-game player's narrative. Virtually everyone I know played Kung-Fu and Double Dribble and Super Mario Brothers on Nintendo. But it took special determination to stick with gaming and move on to the Sega Genesis (which hosted what is still the best hockey game ever made: EA Sports' NHL 97), and it took yet another kind of commitment to hang in there and purchase a Nintendo 64. Here games began to get so complicated that those who abandoned the pastime at the 8-bit Nintendo level were doomed to feel lost. The controllers sprouted carbuncles of new buttons, at the touch of which any number of menus and submenus would slide, drop, or blink onto the screen. The Playstation 2's controller, for instance, has no fewer than seventeen buttons, and games such as Desert Storm II: Back to Baghdad offer such elaborations of command and movement that mastering them fills one with a sense of achievement not unlike playing a piece of complicated music.

• • •

It should be said that, not terribly long ago, the novel was often seen as being indicative of supposed cultural depravity—

before films came along and stole its debauched crown. Video games now seem to be our major briar of cultural entanglement. For better or worse, resistance is a powerful indicator of a given medium's vigor, by that metric, video games are the most powerful cultural force we now have. We are no longer worried that children are missing school because of video games, though. We are worried that they are murdering their classmates because of video games.

Entertainment is not a neutral property. Art, obligated to address questions allergic to mere entertainment, is even less a neutral property. In my humble estimation, no video game has yet crossed the Rubicon from entertainment to true art, but something is happening, and in some of the violent spasms linked to video games we may be seeing the first signs of their eventual growth into something that cares more about story and character than blowing the head off a rival drug lord. They are, in other words, learning what they can do. Nonetheless, the connection between video games and real-life violence remains more sensed than proven. In *The Effect of Videogames on Children: The Myth Unmasked*, U.K. journalism professor Barry Gunter points out several studies' suggestion that video games actually enhance many kids' problem-solving abilities and teach them to think abstractly. Video games without question positively affect measurable abilities such as hand-eye coordination, as I learned when I picked up the banjo a few years ago and found fretting and chord making much easier than I had anticipated. The video-game scholar J. C. Herz, in her landmark book *Joystick Nation*, agrees: "Those to the joystick born have a built-in advantage. . . . They're simply acclimated to a world that increasingly resembles some kind of arcade experience."

This is an interesting debate to be sure, but it is also, in my view, a distraction from the real issue, which is the far more disquieting possibility that video games and other electronic distractions are creating a culture literally afraid of interiority. Literature, of course, values interiority above all. Herz is right: The world *does* increasingly resemble some kind of "arcade experience," but learning to live in an arcade, rather than knowing how to cope while occasionally visiting one, does not seem an appetizing, much less necessary, fate. I do not mean to succumb to Luddite wet-blanketism. After all, I play video games. I also try to be careful. When I play too many video games I begin to feel chubby-minded, caffeinated, *bad*. A mind in constant need of prodding along invisible wavelengths is not a mind I wish to have. Fun is not the same thing as fulfillment. The major problem with video games is that they give us the pleasure of a problem solved without requiring the kind of mental activity normally associated with problem solving. This carries over, in other ways, to similar digital distractions. A recent article in the *New York Times* noted how, ten years ago, teenage commuters in Japan could be counted upon to be reading comics or magazines or even novels; now most amuse themselves by sending out text messages on their cell phones. If one's consciousness is bombarded relentlessly enough, it *can* grow less complex and more easily sated, and the world David Foster Wallace envisioned in *Infinite Jest,* where people *die* entertaining themselves, grows terrifyingly closer to being fulfilled.

Reading, like video games, is both an activity and a cultural phenomenon. Its popularity grows and fades, fades and grows; its human importance is not fixed, and it can be damaged, if not lost forever. But why read? After all, literacy as a pandemic social condition is around three hundred years old. I would argue that reading nourishes and protects one's consciousness. It creates independence of mind (a trait to be valued above all else), fosters skepticism, and, perhaps most important, relieves simple human loneliness. Reading gives one something to think about other than oneself. The rise of literacy in the West and the collapse of despotism and the mortal wounding of Christian fundamentalism are surely not merely a happy coincidence. I will not make the spinachy claim that reading makes one a "better person" (the battlefield of literature is filled with too many psychic casualties for that to be true) or that a nation of readers guarantees social justice and harmony. The wicked can and have been astoundingly literate. But a nation of readers would go some way toward ridding a culture so afflicted by solipsism, parochialism, crudeness, and apathy. Talk to people who do not read for pleasure. Really *talk* to them. Notice the panic in their eyes as you steer the conversation toward anything related to the larger world; note the anger with which they respond to anything that requires them to step outside themselves. Most nonreaders are nothing but an agglomeration of third-hand opinion and blindly received wisdom. Nonreaders are also the majority, and they now have more opportunities than ever to flee even deeper into themselves while still leaving interiority behind.

In 1991, Saul Bellow wrote:

> The modern reader (or viewer, or listener: let's include everybody) is perilously overloaded. . . . Our consciousness is a staging area, a field of operations for all kinds of enterprises, which make free use of it. True, we are at liberty to

think our own thoughts, but our independent ideas, such as they may be, must live with thousands of ideas and notions inculcated by influential teachers, or floated by "idea men," advertisers, communications people, columnists, anchormen, et cetera. Better-regulated (educated) minds are less easily overcome by these gas clouds of opinion. But no one can have an easy time of it. In all fields we are forced to seek special instruction, expert guidance to the interpretation of the seeming facts we are stuffed with. This is in itself a full-time occupation. . . . Vast organizations exist to get our attention. They make cunning plans. They bite us with their ten-second bites. Our consciousness is their staple; they live on it. Think of consciousness just opening to settlement and exploitation, something like an Oklahoma land rush. Put it in color, set it to music, frame it in images—but even this fails to do justice to the vision. Obviously consciousness is infinitely bigger than Oklahoma.

Every literary person, then, is a conservationist in the fight for increasingly endangered consciousness. Antitechnology radicalism is not the answer to this endangerment, and neither is dourness about phenomena such as video games. But an enjoyment or even love of digital distraction needs fortification with something that appreciates and rewards the inner life. Without such fortification one is wading in the shallow end of an intellectual kiddie pool.

Any talk of "rewarding the inner life" admittedly sounds very Merchant and Ivory, very highfalutin. Our generation largely distrusts the highfalutin, a stance that has its benefits and deficits. One benefit is our suspicion of those who assume that a coming tribe of televisual zombies with the attention span of puppies will be the very doom of literary culture. Every literary generation has had its distractions, some far more toxic than video games—often literally so. Hemingway, for instance, had booze, broads, and big-game hunting. Fitzgerald had booze, screenwriting, and his wife's insanity. Surely Hemingway's and Fitzgerald's distractions brought them a little more wisdom and worldly engagement than getting past the eleventh board of The Getaway, but it would be hard to argue that it made them more productive writers. (I sincerely doubt that either one of them would have been capable of getting past the eleventh board of The Getaways, at any rate.)

All writers waste time in innumerable ways. Gambling, shopping, football on a Sunday afternoon, sex, food: None are without their pleasures, or torments, and none are necessarily conducive to a literary life. The end of Rabbit, Run finds Updike's eponymous hero running from his spouse, his dead child, his life, while "he feels his insides as very real suddenly, a pure blank space in the middle of a dense net." Rabbit Angstrom's distraction is something as square as basketball. Without it, he is nothing. How strange that a book about a young man losing track of himself allowed me to find myself. And how wonderful that, today, it reminds me that it does not matter, in the end, what distracts us. What matters is what we make of our distractions. Or choose not to make. Some distractions are merely distractions.

IF I HAD A STAMMER

Meghan Daum

A funny thing happened on the way to turning thirty-five. As though tripping on a string of Christmas lights that had edged themselves out of a dusty basement corner, I began losing battles in my war with sentimentality. These are the sorts of battles you don't always realize you've lost until the new regime has taken over and ordered a new china pattern. It's a nearly imperceptible series of defeats; first you cry at weddings, then you cry at the General Electric commercials that play during *Meet the Press*, then you both cry and laugh at what you suddenly perceive to be the great verbal acumen and emotional range of Calvin Trillin.

If that sequence of events reads to you like a list of warning signs to degenerative illness you are probably (a) under thirty and (b) absolutely within your rights as an under-thirty person to regard such sentimentality as tantamount to beholding a twenty- by forty-foot painting by Thomas Kinkaid, the Six Million Dollar Man of impressionism, and saying, "Now *that's* art." You have also (c) probably spent too much time in used-record stores and/or listening to public radio. How do I know? I can hear it in your voice (and in mine).

For reasons I will go to my grave trying to unpack (when you don't have a mind for physics you're left with this), there is now an entire class of people who have come to express their social and cultural pedigree through a particular kind of vocal intonation. In fact, if there is any hallmark of my generation's literary sensibility, I'm inclined to believe it is not what we commit to paper but how we expel the words from our mouths. If such a concept as *our literature* exists, it does so in the form of the spoken word—not only in the spoken word genre but in everyday speech patterns, the manner in which we order eggs off a menu, the sounds of our voices on answering machines.

Call it the Stammering Class. Call it the Nasal Academy. Call it the sonic manifestation of affluence and postmodernism, the love child of Reaganomics and Grunge. The counterpoint to the much maligned, teenaged-girl-dominated "up talk," this intonation takes anything ending in the upward sweeping sound of a question mark and flicks it onto the ground as though it were a fly. It is, for lack of a better term, *down talk*. The official tongue of hipsters, lesbians, and anyone whose voice has ever been heard on National Public Radio, it manages to convey a supreme sense of casualness while also taking itself very, very seriously. It sails over phrases like "cultural context" and "grass-roots effort" as though such phrases exist only within the utopian region of down talk's dialect. Its sentences bask in the speaker's lack of amusement, capturing the romantic disenchantment of the English major for whom Salinger has suddenly lost his allure (brainier down talkers will worship Salinger in high school but lose interest by college, ditto for Vonnegut, Kerouac, and Henry Miller). However, down talkers, no matter how obscure their tastes become, will never cease to worship William Burroughs.

This is a complicated business to suss out. For one thing, as you no doubt noticed, I am engaged in the rather futile exercise of writing about voice modulation rather than talking about it. If I sat before you now, I'd show you myself. I'd talk down talk to you. I'd press my tongue hard against that ridge of gum just above the inside of the upper teeth (for some reason, this is for me the proper starting position for the swan dive into down talk) and explain to you, you know, what the deal is.

Instead, the airwaves must suffice. Turn on the public or college station and listen for ten minutes. You will hear this literature on the hipper, fringier programs. Ironic music will toodle in the background, long pauses will leave discomfiting blank spaces. Upon occasion you will hear us reporting from the field, not from the front lines of wars or political campaigns but from the frontiers of American quirkdom. We're the ones who tell you about the mom-and-pop groceries closing in Baton Rouge. We're who tells you about a guy who rides a Segway Human Transporter over the Rocky Mountains, the Dalmatian that only responds to commands in Farsi, and just about anything that takes place in Seattle. You will hear us drop our voices at the end of sentences as if to suggest that what we're saying, even if it concerns a Pillsbury bake-off, is a humanitarian crisis of genocidal proportions. You will hear us swallowing our words so that our syllables have the texture of lava rocks; call it vox gravelax. The words gurgle in the back of the throat like a boiling pot of ramen noodles. This is the sound of the ultimate seriousness brought to you by the folks from the ultimate casualness. Down talk is always measured, even sluggish, like an LP spinning just slightly too slow. The vowels are as attenuated as El Greco figures, screaming for mercy as we reach for the next word.

The flat, treeless plains of down talk's terrain are nicked only by one notable variation in the topography, the chronic stammer. The richer, more glamorous cousin of the stutter, the stammer is the must-have accessory for the down talker who wants that little something extra in the intellectual department. Despite reflecting none of the political or cultural tastes of his tonal predecessors, the great down talker William F. Buckley set a stammering standard that is now carried out in world-class style by public radio personalities like Terry Gross and Ira Glass, both of whom are major heroes in the down-talking community. And who can blame us? Stammering is this literature's antiminimalism, spoken word's answer to hypographia. The verbal equivalent to descending a staircase two steps at a time, the stammer suggests that the speaker has so much to say there isn't time to get all the words in. He is at once so unrehearsed and possessed of such a large vocabulary that the process of choosing a word is as overwhelming as devising a national health care system. He has all the makings of a literary genius, even if he's never written a word.

Riding the coattails of tortured vowels' spit-producing stammers is one of the linguistic bedrocks of down talk, the construction "very sort of." In the last six months, I have heard "very sort of" used no less than forty-five times, at least thirty-seven of those usages occurring at bookstores, literary events, or coffee shops on to whose tip jars are taped little notes reading "support counter intelligence." Members of the stammering class, particularly those who feel pressure to hold opinions about the arts while not alienating the creators of the art, who may be standing behind them at the gallery opening, find "very sort of" to be just the ticket.

"Wilco's latest album is very sort of experimental, but not overly so."

"I always find Riesling to be very sort of twee."

"I feel very sort of hungover this morning. It must have been those six shots of Everclear."

In the world of down talk, people with multiple graduate degrees see no semantic conflict in characterizing everything from Ikea sleeper sofas to the art of floral arrangement as "very sort of, like, Zen." Most people use "very sort of" when they really mean "not even remotely like" ("Laurel Canyon is very sort of Haight-Ashbury in the eighties with foliage."). Most often, however, "very sort of" is a place holder for nothingness. I would bet money that a detailed linguistic survey of the usage of "very sort of" would show that it's almost always a way of saying, "I don't know what to say about this." In French, that would be *je ne sais quoi*, but resorting to French is very sort of . . . 1980s.

Though fancying itself the exact opposite of bourgeois pretension, down talk is primarily about social class. It is a speech pattern that reveals not only economic status and region but tastes and hobbies and political affiliation. Down talk, like eating disorders and Botox, is most often found in the middle and upper middle class. It is rarely spoken by political conservatives, even less often by those who enjoy sports. Though down talk can appear rooted in white culture by virtue of its lackluster sheen and mashed-potato-like texture, any ethnicity is free to adapt it, though for some reason Asians do so in greater proportions than blacks or Latinos. As I mentioned earlier, lesbians, at least many of them, must carry a gene for down talk—and lucky them! In the clutches of down talk's lock-jawed, simmering intensity, every statement, even one involving handbags, is a *political statement*. Down talk is an express train to being taken seriously, so who wouldn't want to take it? It is possible to combine down talk with a southern accent (most notably the Austin, Texas, Athens, Georgia, or Oxford, Mississippi, varieties) but entirely impossible to do so with a prominent New York, New Jersey, or Boston accent. Californians and midwesterners are at an advantage in this arena, their native accents having prechewed their words into the mealy syllables on which down talk thrives. Most college students, but especially those majoring in the liberal arts, will experiment with down talk as readily as with marijuana (indeed the latter is a mighty enhancer of the former). Like schizophrenia, down talk most commonly presents itself in one's early twenties. It is rare to hear it from any but the most precocious teenagers. It is even rarer for it to develop afresh in anyone over twenty-five. As with mental illness, once a person has been afflicted with this voice modulation, it is nearly impossible to achieve a complete cure.

And so I return to down talk's arch enemy, sentimentality. If down talk is Ira Glass and Wilco and much of the literature that appears in the many fine, small literary magazines being published today, sentimentality is Diane Sawyer and Celine Dion and nine out of ten fiction titles on the best seller lists of America. If down talk is the cultural elite, then sentimentality is everyone else, the hard-working men and women of this country, the people who listen to AM radio because ostensibly they still haven't figured out that FM exists. Welcome to the two Americas. But the problem is that that's not true. There are not two Americas but something closer to 250 million Americas. The problem with down talk, with this emotional literature so many of us adore, is that it masquerades as an expression of individualism when it is, in fact, about as generic as the linens aisle at Target (down talkers love Target, incidentally, and not even in a campy way).

So this is why I can no longer listen to certain public radio programs without wanting to send a giant box of throat lozenges to every local affiliate in the country. I can no longer buy a latte, an old Clash record, or, for that matter, a piece of handmade jewelry without being made to feel that I am participating in some kind of franchise of coolness. This isn't because I'm not a fan of irony—when that day comes I'll have to relinquish my black-framed glasses, rendering myself blind—but because down talk somehow manages to undermine genuine irony by letting voice modulation steal the show. With down talk, every utterance becomes ironic. Office chitchat starts to sound like banter on Comedy Central. You can't order pancakes in a diner without causing the waitress to wonder if you really mean it. Moreover, everything upon everything—from making a dinner reservation to purchasing a can of paint thinner at the hardware store—takes on the stammering, lackadaisical qualities of a certain kind of voice on National Public Radio. Or at least that's what happened when I made a dinner reservation and bought paint thinner earlier today. What's most interesting to me about this "literature" is the power wielded by the very fact of its not being literature at all. By seeping into our consciousness like an invisible gas, it does what more definable categories of culture (for instance, books) simply cannot do; it does the work for us. It make us seem sincere when we may be lying and smart when we may be stupid. Even better, it make us bookish without our actually having to read.

Talk about best-selling stuff. How very sort of brilliant.

PUTTING GAY FICTION
BACK TOGETHER

K. M. Soehnlein

There was a time when gay fiction mattered.

From the mid to late 1980s through the early to mid 1990s, a confluence of factors elevated gay fiction into prominence: an "out" population demanding political recognition, a readership dependent upon books for honest depictions of their lives, a national network of gay bookstores, and a publishing industry courting this emerging market. This was a time when gay writers understood their mission in the grandest terms: to hold up a mirror, but at a slant, so that the angle of reflection would capture not just the newly visible self but the surrounding world as well. Gay fiction would tell stories that had not yet been told, and tell them well. Gay fiction would make gay lives the stuff of literature.

In 1991, Edmund White, one of the genre's pioneers, began an article in the *New York Times Magazine* noting that "the revolution of the gay male novel has seemed breathlessly rapid." He recounted an event at the 1991 Out/Write conference in San Francisco, when playwright Edward Albee was booed by a predominantly gay and lesbian audience for asserting that he would not be saddled with the label "gay writer." I was at that jam-packed assembly and remember well the frustration felt by the crowd. Here we were, young, proud, and galvanized, and one of the old guard was wagging his finger at us for the very thing that bound us together. It was one of those volatile public moments that felt instantly important, history in the making.

A couple years ago, I attended the Lambda Literary Conference, the descendant of Out/Write, again held in San Francisco. The three-day event was cordial, intimate, networky, and devoid of even the slightest whiff of controversy, more a class reunion than a public brawl. Indeed, when it comes to gay literature, what is there to fight about? Ten years after White's essay appeared, you'd be hard-pressed to find the *Times Magazine* exploring the gay male novel as a cultural topic, much less one in a state of breathless revolution.

What happened? How did we go from volatile to humdrum in little more than a decade?

Before the 1970s, there was no "gay fiction," no section of the literary landscape staked out by writers, pitched to publishers, and sold to readers under this name. Literary novels with gay characters and themes—*The Well of Loneliness, The City and the Pillar, The Sexual Outlaw*—existed singly, like small island states blotching a vast, indifferent sea of books. Such works were labeled by their publishers as "controversial" or "shocking," which was a way to titillate readers who were not gay or lesbian, rather than connect to those who were.

That the concept of "gay fiction" was new, even revolutionary, was not something I understood, coming out at college in the mid-1980s, when novels illuminating this life I had claimed were already available to me. These novels captured the perspectives of self-identified gay men, revealed the history of their long-silent subculture, depicted the sex that they were having (the kind of sex I was starting to have). This knowledge was not available through movies, TV, or high school health class, only through the intimacy of the printed page.

These were the worst of times for gay men, when the Reagan administration set policy to please its fundamentalist Christian cronies; when a squeamish Supreme Court decided the Constitution didn't protect consensual sex if the mouth or ass was involved; when HIV was decimating us. But it was also the best of times. Two decades earlier gay men found each other only in bars and at cruising spots, went to psychiatrists to turn straight, and kept their mouths shut in public. That there was now an aboveground gay community, with its own social organizations, businesses, and newspapers—that gay bars might now have windows that let in light—was a kind of miracle. Vito Russo, author of *The Celluloid Closet*, said of coming out, "The truth will set you free, but first it will make you miserable." During those best and worst of times, literature was my bridge between misery and freedom.

I can chart my coming of age according to the novels I read at that time: the desire stirred up by Patricia Nell Warren's steamy romance, *The Front Runner*, when such longing was still taboo to me; the identification I felt with the high school protagonist of John Fox's *Boys on the Rock*, who spends the first part of the book trying to convince everyone, even the reader, that he's fucking Sue when it's Al he's hot for, but ultimately gains the self-assurance to send the half-closeted Al packing; the struggle of a mother to come to terms with her son's gayness in Laura Z. Hobson's *Consenting Adult*, a copy of which I gave to my own mother and which brought out her empathy more than the self-help title (*Now That You Know*) I'd earlier foisted on her. When I moved to New York after college, I found my footing in downtown gay life by reading John Weir's *The Irreversible Decline of Eddie Socket*, Gary Indiana's *Horse Crazy*, and Sarah Schulman's *People in Trouble*. Alan Hollinghurst's *Swimming Pool Library* was very British but spoke to me with its unbridled sex and its journey into pre-Stonewall gay history; Jeanette Winterson's *The Passion* was very British *and* lesbian but still served as a tool of seduction between me and the boy I fell for.

Books were necessary, and writers—as that outcry over Albee reinforces—were looked up to. Writers, in fact, were all we had. Aside from a couple of politicians, writers were the only openly gay public figures. Even the celebrity icons we take for granted today—Martina Navratilova, Elton John—were in the closet back then.

The situation was so ripe that by 1994, in his introduction to *Waves: An Anthology of New Gay Fiction*, editor Ethan Mordden was able to argue that two "waves" of gay fiction had already come and gone. The first was centered on the Violet Quill, a small circle of cultured New Yorkers including Edmund White (*A Boy's Own Story*), Andrew Holleran (*Dancer from the Dance)*, and Felice Picano (*The Lure*), who met regularly for a few years in the late 1970s and early 1980s, and whose cumulative writings helped put gay fiction on the map. This was the Stonewall generation; indeed, Edmund White was at the Stonewall Inn, a Greenwich Village gay bar, the night the patrons rebelled against a police raid. The Violet Quill has come to symbolize for gay literature what Stonewall has for gay politics: the crucible that enabled what followed.

The second wave Mordden identified was made up of the disparate authors who emerged in the mid-1980s, like David Leavitt (*Family Dancing*), Dennis Cooper (*Closer*), and Stephen McCauley (*The Object of My Affection*), who built upon the Violet Quill's publishing successes but branched out beyond their urban concerns and urbane aesthetics. A third wave, Mordden wrote, was emerging from a generation—my generation—that was "political, archetypal, experimental." This was exciting news for me, already at work on a novel of my own, ready to catch that wave and ride it hard.

Alas, it crashed offshore. Of the authors included in Mordden's anthology, only Michael Cunningham—who won the 1999 Pulitzer for *The Hours*—has gone on to indisputable literary success. John Weir hasn't written a second novel; Scott Heim last published one in 1997; Jim Provenzano's two novels have been self-published at much personal expense and effort. And then there's Brad Gooch, who abandoned serious fiction (*The Golden Age of Promiscuity*) and scholarship (*City Poet: The Life and Times of Frank O'Hara*) for self-help, penning *The Boyfriend Within* and *Dating the Greek Gods*, brisk-selling dating manuals that seem to promise a lover as handsome as the author, whose face beams from each cover.

"Gay fiction doesn't sell." This was the argument heard again and again by my agent, shopping my novel around to publishers in 1999. Too many big advances had not been earned back by gay books in the previous decade. My own bookshelves bear this story out, lined as they are with slashed-price copies of mid-1990s works by queer fiction pioneers like Holleran and White. Gay fiction, hyped as the next big thing, was being remaindered. Today, no major New York publisher is cultivating a list of gay male authors; of the midsize houses, only Alyson and Kensington (the eventual buyer of my novel) are doing so. Compare that to the late 1980s, when one imprint alone, NAL/Dutton's Plume, boasted thirty queer fiction titles.

What happened in the 1990s to gay fiction is, in part, what happened to all fiction. Sales dropped, corporate mergers reorganized publishers around the bottom line, and the one-two punch of online booksellers and chain store expansion toppled bricks-and-mortar independent retailers. (Gay bookstores went dark in New York, Los Angeles, Boston, and many other cities.) Recent studies tell us that those under thirty-five are half as likely as those thirty-five and older to read a single novel or book of poetry in a year. Young gays and lesbians seeking a sense of connectedness are thus less likely to look for it in a book than on a screen of one size or another, where they will surely find something. The television industry realized several years ago that homosexuals could be packaged for primetime, usually in soaps (*Melrose Place*) or sitcoms (*Ellen*); today, cable TV is full of same-sex kissing, and most reality shows designate a token queer slot. If such glossy, market-driven portrayals don't satisfy, you can communicate directly with someone just like yourself through an online community—one without a

center but easily accessed, disembodied but talking amongst itself all the time. What was once available only from a trip to
the nearest big city (often not so near) now comes and finds
you behind your own closed door.

All these changes in media and technology took place in
tandem with one more: the introduction of protease in-
hibitors, the AIDS drugs that gave people with HIV a future.
This scientific breakthrough has had a very specific, but rarely
discussed, effect on gay literature. For fifteen years, gay men,
including too many writers and editors, died in droves. The
mortal truths ushered in by this plague became the stuff of our
literature. Thus the gay male novel became the AIDS novel,
its "revolution" mired in night sweats, bedpans, and eulogies.

Then AIDS was corralled, but novels concerned with its effects, already in the production pipeline, continued to appear.
Gay readers began to walk away from our grim fictional tales
and have not yet looked back. (Having been given new life,
they obsess about lifestyle, evidenced by a glut of books on dé-
cor, dating, and physique.) Allan Gurganus's *Plays Well with
Others*—to my thinking, the most elegant depiction in prose of
how the plague transformed a generation—should have been
regarded as one of the masterpieces of gay literature, of *all* contemporary literature, when it appeared in 1997. Dismissed as an
"AIDS novel" after AIDS stopped showing up on the nightly
news, it became one of those big books on the remainder table.
The publishing industry determined that our fiction wasn't selling, and gay writers were left scrambling for subject matter.

Gay fiction today is an art form dismantled, a pie chart of
subgenres: romance, horror, mystery, humor. There's a preponderance of "lit-lite," the stuff with gossip in its veins, promising

readers a backstage look at Hollywood, the fashion industry, the social circles of moneyed Manhattan. Gay bookstores overflow with specialized anthologies; a recent edition of the monthly *Lambda Book Report*, a must-read for gay authors, lists calls for entries for works on "true stories from leatherbars," "how bi-men come out," "black lesbian stories of longing, lust and love," "queer writers discussing their attachment to a different race, religion, nationality, etc.," "working class themes" and "gay travels in Islam." These books put specialized content first, almost ensuring that the *quality* of the writing will be a second priority. Taken together, anthologies like these paint a picture of a community so splintered it can barely relate to itself, much less comment on the outside world.

Similarly, more and more queer bookstore shelves are filled with "erotica," a relatively new designation straddling the line between fiction and nonfiction. (Is anyone really fact-checking how "true" those "stories from leatherbars" really are?) Erotica supposedly serves as a testament that pornography has gotten intelligent, even artful, though my own readings in the genre have turned up many stories so focused on the money shot they engage the imagination no more deeply than porn (and many too silly to even get the blood pumping). Though a frank depiction of sex has always been one of the pioneering aspects of gay fiction, gay fiction has never been just about sex. Erotica seems to me like most of the new gay subgenres, a retreat. Gay lit without the lit.

Erotica is sex as entertainment; on the other side of the coin is gay writing that provides entertainment with no sex. Here we find today's most successful openly gay author, David Sedaris, whose memoirs recount a faggy childhood and a domestic, boyfriend-centered adult life, all the while steering clear of sex. In a recent interview he noted, "On the lecture tours, you say the word 'I' when you read out loud, and people would imagine me having sex. It is not pleasant for people to imagine me having sex." Only a writer who sees himself first and foremost as a performer would decide what goes into his books based on how it will present from a podium. Indeed, Sedaris began on the radio; his work on the page almost demands that you have already heard him speak. Sedaris is hilarious, but he is an entertainer, not a model for the resuscitation of gay writing.

Michael Cunningham might be. Possibly the most respected author to emerge from gay fiction's heyday, Cunningham has consistently remained true to his original vision. He's done this in part by working slowly but steadily, producing three novels in ten years—*A Home at the End of the World, Flesh and Blood,* and *The Hours.* His "queer eye" takes in everyone: gay, straight, and in between; male, female, and transgender. (A lack of female characters is one of the shortcomings of gay male fiction; you can't hold a mirror to the world and reflect only men.) In Cunningham's fiction, intimate events in the lives of gay characters reveal society's larger story. His novels span decades, but every moment, every sentence, every image is rendered with God-in-the-details precision.

The best gay fiction of the last few years—Jamie O'Neill's *At Swim, Two Boys;* Allan Gurganus's *The Practical Heart;* Trebor Healey's *Through It Came Bright Colors*—shares this careful crafting. These authors neither shy away from sex nor assert it at the expense of characterization, language, or story. Each of these works points toward how the various strands of contemporary gay literature, subdivided and specialized across bookstore shelves, might be reassembled into works that are meaningful and integral, held together not just by (sub)cultural content but by artistic form—by the union of the two, the writer's voice, the foundation of any fiction worth talking about.

If worthy novels by gay male writers are still being published, does it matter that the category has lost its prominence? One can argue that such a situation is preferable, a sign of political assimilation. Perhaps we have come full circle to Edward Albee, whose desire to be seen as simply a writer, without the delineating modifier *gay*, no longer seems heretical but status quo. One thinks of the oft-used construction "so-and-so *happens* to be gay," which treats homosexuality as a trait no more significant than left-handedness. But, of course, left-handers are no longer shamed into altering their natural dexterity; homosexuals still start out their lives presumed by everyone around them not to be homosexual. A minority culture, misunderstood and seen as alien (to say nothing of the rights denied it), needs its own literature. Gay fiction may have lost some of its necessary social function, but what has stepped in to replace it is grossly inadequate. On *Will and Grace*, sexuality is a joke, funny ha-ha when mentioned on-screen and funny-strange in its implication. The best-written gay characters on TV, David and Keith on *Six Feet Under*, occupy the opposite end of the spectrum: a world without any other gay men except those with whom they have passing sex.

I take some comfort in an emerging new "wave" of gay fiction. It includes those of us who could have been third-wavers ten years ago but took too long, and those emerging since, largely at smaller presses and university imprints (Southern Tier, Graywolf, Soft Skull, Suspect Thoughts, Green Candy, University of Wisconsin, Cleis). These are the new publishing heroes of gay—or, more accurately, more inclusively—*queer* fiction. They have taken up the slack left by the big New York houses, whose relevance has diminished as strategies of corporate "synergy" diminish the possibility of real risk taking. That's the good news. The bad news is that these smaller presses rarely have the distribution or deep pockets that enable writers to make a viable living, a problem not just for individual authors but for literary culture.

However these commercial forces shake out, the challenge remains for gay writers to recommit to this identity while telling the largest story possible. Not "large" in terms of sweeping casts of characters and swaths of history, though such expansiveness is ours to claim, but in terms of the ideas only we can offer, the perspective only our mirrors will afford. Gay fiction will matter again when our writers see themselves as not only necessary to the articulation of the queer experience, but also necessary to the future of literature.

VOICE OF A GENERATION

Paul Flores

If it hadn't been for Governor Pete Wilson, I might have never become a spoken word artist.

The year was 1994, and anti-immigrant hysteria was running rampant through the California legislature and on AM radio waves, blaming the state's dire economic situation on costs related to servicing undocumented workers. According to Governor Wilson "illegal immigrants" didn't pay income taxes. So not only were they stealing money from California, but it was costing the state whenever an undocumented child was educated in a public school, or whenever a doctor delivered a Mexican baby. I was a college student in San Diego at the time (thanks to affirmative action), and Proposition 187 had been passed, denying immigrants the right to public education and health services (including the emergency room), and also encouraging snitching on "suspected" noncitizens. It was the first piece of legal racism that directly crossed my path. It would be followed by Propositions 227 and 209, which removed bilingual education and affirmative action from public schools and government hiring. In response to this personal attack on my family, I began to write about what my grandfather had done to exchange his life of poverty in Mexico for that of an American steel worker, now retired in California.

I wrote about how dark his skin was, how he wore long-sleeved shirts and a sombrero, how he went back to school at the age of forty to get an American high school diploma. I wrote of my teenage cousin Tommy being sent to secondary at the San Onofre immigration checkpoint because he was *moreno*, a dark-skinned Mexican. I wrote a poem that could be used as a weapon to combat those who would deny my family the rights of citizenship and the rewards of their labor. It was the first poem I ever read at a Chicano open mike. I was twenty-two years old, and I had finally figured something out about myself.

> *I could see/Mexicans running/into themselves/into their*
> *   padres/into their compadres/*
> *into life they want returned/into their*
> *   tierra/desconocida/aislada/matada/running to a home they*
> *   know/en sus corazones que/it's theirs without papers.*
>
> ("VISTA," 1994)

It was amazing. And it was just the beginning. By sharing my own experience and connecting it to a larger issue, I became part of a much larger movement. I began performing spoken word both to have a voice and articulate injustices. Ten years later, I make my living in San Francisco and perform in cities all over the world, connecting my personal narrative not only to a specific community, but also to an entire generation. Young people, and Latinos in particular, are what Antonio Gramsci defined as subaltern: "groups left out of established structures of representation." I believe that the spoken word movement is uniquely capable of reaching out to these segments of the population that still stand on the margins.

I realized a long time ago through my own work, and through mentoring young writers, that there is no speech without freedom. In other words, the best way to defeat stereotypes and empower the disenfranchised is to offer the tools of language so that we can re-create our existence in the most authentic way possible. How can you ask someone to take responsibility for his or her actions in words that don't reflect his or her experience or understanding?

You can't. In 1996 I began working at Youth Speaks (www .youthspeaks.org), a nonprofit organization in San Francisco devoted to creating safe, uncensored spaces for teenagers interested in creative writing and spoken word, because I wanted to feel part of a community of writers. I had previously enrolled in a standard MFA program, and heading to departmental and local poetry readings was no longer satisfying me. The readings were stuffy and pompous for no reason I could understand. I did know, however, that I was usually one of only three people of color in the room, and if you hadn't published a book, no one really paid attention to you. So when James Kass, the director of Youth Speaks, asked me if I wanted to visit high schools to perform poems and lead after-school workshops for San Francisco youth, I was excited and motivated. This was the person I wanted to be: a literary activist, a mentor, a spoken word poet, an important part of something new.

I had already been working with Los Delicados, a touring group of Latino spoken word and theater formed out of the San Francisco State University writing program, which I had attended. But it wasn't until I began working with the young writers at Youth Speaks that I learned the full potential spoken word contains. These teen poets taught me. They weren't impressed by my MFA. They wanted to know if I could "bust" in the classroom as well as onstage. They helped guide my voice toward honesty. I couldn't fake my words or force my leadership skills; I couldn't pretend I was somebody I wasn't. This is what I had wanted from the instructors and writers in the MFA program; and instead I found it in these teenagers. They challenged me, and in the process I found the perfect intersection of my art and my politics.

> *My language is STRONG like struggle./Sorry if*
> *I curse, but my mother worked all day/*
> *and I was on my own after school/a latchkey kid*
> *kicking it behind the 7/11/drinking brew, listening*
> *to Ice Cube/"Since I was a youth I smoked weed*
> *out/Now I'm the motherf* * *er that you read*
> *about."/I used to like to fight and shout obscenities/*
> *to get attention./There was no man around the*
> *house,/except THE MAN./Who knew me and*
> *my mom so well/I had to change my last name/just so*
> *people wouldn't think my dad was a cop./So I became*
> *like Cyrano's Chicano twin/ and bled la vida loca*
> *from my pen.*
>
> ("MY LANGUAGE," 2003, WITH QUOTE
> FROM NWA "F#@K THA POLICE")

Hip-hop is central to the whole project. I am part of the generation that grew up with hip-hop, and that participated in its development, so I reference rap and hip-hop history in my work. Many Youth Speaks poets feel they have more in common with Tupac or Lauryn Hill, than Robert Frost or Maya Angelou. So I sing and I rhyme, I evoke MCs when I'm on the mike. I give props to hip-hop because it tells the gritty story of my generation—of urban Latinos and blacks growing up economically segregated, bitter, and easily manipulated by all that we never had: money, clothes, cars, access, respect, a nuclear family, status. But hip-hop held transcendental power for us, it was our creative burst that took us beyond those psychological and class-determined limits and into mainstream culture.

I also got that MFA in creative writing, even though the program failed to inspire me. Which means I have studied the history of poetry, its forms, its trends, its styles, and I have read the so-called masters of the Western canon. I am thankful for this training because it gave me time to experiment until I found my own poetic voice, which I realized was decidedly nonacademic, noninstitutional. I don't want to be like Mark Strand, or T. S. Eliot. I write for a different purpose and a different audience. It is necessary to read Strand's and Elliot's poetry on the page in order to understand it, because some of the abstractions are meant to be deciphered through close reading. I, on the other hand, seek continuity with oral tradition.

A pure, transparent, rhythmic storytelling—and always with a narrative structure—is the kind of poetry I write and perform. Immediate reaction and connection to a live audience, as in much of early hip-hop, is the goal. I want action. I want group dialogue. I want call and response. I want community. I want artistic movement for our generation.

It sounds utopian, but I'm not going to let that stop me. I was recently in Miami on a residency teaching spoken word to young people in East Little Havana. Most of them were either Latino immigrants or the children of immigrants. They suffered multiple issues of racial and cultural identity confusion: Were they black or Latino? Hispanic or "American"? Victims or criminals? We attempted to clarify some of their problems by writing poems about ancestry, home, social status, and assimilation. Committing to an identity by these means—or perhaps at all—was still too complicated for some. But more than anything else, they all responded to hip-hop.

They understood the language of hip-hop. They knew what *fresh* meant, *crunk, ice,* and *shorty.* They could expound on the merits of Tupac, Biggie, and Eminem. In short, they knew exactly where they stood in relationship to this medium of expression. Many of them were not fluent in English, but they could recognize the rhythmic patterns of rap as if it was their mother's *gallo pinto* and *carne asada.* I encouraged them to use hip-hop and Spanglish in their writing so that they could feel as if the poetry they wrote was indeed theirs, and not the tradition of dead white men. I told them spoken word was done with the language they already had on their tongue: It was the voice in their head, natural, organic, and true to their experience.

> *You don't know me/You think I am a hoochie because of*
> *what I wear/You think I always lose/ but at least I intend*
> *to try/You think I will have a lot of children/because my*

great-grandmother had ten/You think I am worthless/but
I am worth more than what you wear//
  I don't care what you think/I know I can dance until my
    feet fall off/I know I can play good soccer and score three
    goals/I know how to make spicy food that will make you
    lick your fingers/and I know I will raise my children
    perfectly well.

                                    (JUANA, FOURTEEN, MIAMI, FLORIDA)

The workshop took off after that, and before long I had a roomful of teenage Spanglish rappers and spoken word artists ready to bust about why country music was so "square" and reggaeton was hot, how dreams were nothing until you actualized them, how the police harassed them for no reason other than being brown in numbers, and whether getting rich was the answer to all of their problems.

Spoken word is the voice of this generation. It is how we connect to the oral/aural messengers of the past: the griots, the storytellers, the shamans, the folksingers, the MCs and rappers. But it is also one way we are going to ensure active literacy in our future. I would like to reach people who can't even read, and show them that they still have a voice, a means to express themselves, a means to dialogue creatively, to criticize, to construct a reality with words that isn't dependent on any institutional validation or degree. This is the populism of spoken word.

To pick up Gramsci again, I think of it as my own subaltern project. This past September I appeared on Def Poetry on HBO, and shared a poem about the military's manipulation of citizenship and college tuition money for immigrant youth who end up dying in Iraq. Thanks to Russell Simmons, and to the overall rise in the popularity of hip-hop and spoken word, I have found a way to use the media to vocalize what the media often ignores.

They say that history is told by the victors. But there is always a struggle over who gets the right to tell the story of the past, and who gets to articulate the events of the present. Spoken word empowers the subaltern, the otherwise ignored, to "tell it like it is." It prioritizes the individual "testimonial" voice. It creates a continuity of artistic languages, such as hip-hop or Spanglish, identity politics, race and culture, into a single art form. Above all, spoken word brings all of these elements together not just for entertainment, but for a greater political and social purpose. Spoken word can help build an identity into a positive force, exemplifying community activism with artistic means. The fact that it is garnering so much interest is a sign that our generation is coming of age.

For more information about teaching hip-hop and poetry to youth, check out *Hip-Hop Poetry and the Classics* by Alan Sitomer and Michael Cirelli (Milk Mug Publishing, 2004); or check out the Youth Speaks wealth of hip-hop-inspired spoken-word books and CDs at www.youthspeaks.org.

AMBASSADORS

Nell Freudenberger

1.

The first time my father visited a communist country was in 1962, when he was seventeen. He recorded his impressions of the trip, which he took with his parents to Yugoslavia and Hungary, in a journal I found recently in my grandmother's basement, on top of a derelict Ping-Pong table. The journal was in an envelope with several generations of passports, some bearing seventy-five-year-old stamps—Greek, Palestinian, and Egyptian—in the same refined palette of blue, green, and ochre. In spite of its stiff maroon leather cover and formal antique font, my paternal great-grandparents' passport, issued May 13, 1929, is a fairly relaxed document. At that time, smack between the wars and a safe six months before the Crash, the two of them carried a joint passport, bearing a youthful portrait (my great-grandmother's hair is bobbed) and the endorsement "good for travel in all countries unless otherwise limited." It seems to stop just short of a breezy "Have a swell time."

By the time my grandparents took my father to the Eastern bloc, American passports had changed. The three of them still traveled on a family passport, but its jacket was now green, patterned with the seal of the U.S. Department of State. It's dated March 13, 1956, and there are a host of new restrictions: "This passport is not valid for travel to Albania, Bulgaria, China, Czechoslovakia, Hungary, Poland, Rumania or the Union of Soviet Socialist Republics" nor for "those portions of Korea and Viet-Nam under Communist control," although in my grandparents' case this portion of the passport had been stamped, "Void." The picture taken of the three of them shows my grandfather, with his characteristic expression of wary disapproval; my grandmother, bright and a bit dazed; and my father behind them, in a plaid shirt with a white undershirt showing, looking somehow (at age eleven) as if he knows the future—as if he's part of some other photograph taken years later, after the world has changed.

Six years after that photograph was taken, they drove from Munich to Budapest, making an "uneventful crossing of the Iron Curtain" at the Hungarian border, where my father noted "barbed wire, cleared strips, armed guards, and a patrol plane":

> When we stopped for an old-fashioned steam locomotive at a crossing, two shorts-clad boys edged up to the car to look in and were promptly motioned away by an Hungarian-speaking man, apparently an official of the communist government (riding alone in a red convertible). They came back and got two pieces of American chewing gum, which one quickly put into his pocket to

make sure it was not taken away from him. But he promised to share it with his friend. They waved something to us as we left and said something about "Amerikanishe." This is the first time we have ever felt that we were ambassadors making an impression in virgin territory.

When I asked his permission to quote from this journal, my father sighed. "It's full of smug, teenaged assertions about the evils of communism, isn't it?"

My father's first impressions (meticulously recorded with the new Adler portable typewriter he'd bought in Germany, on tissue-thin blue stationary from the British Overseas Airlines Corporation) are observant, occasionally smug, and very rarely "teenaged" by any current standard. Reading them for the first time, I marveled at how old-fashioned they sounded; the second time, I wondered how different they were from my own impressions of communism, as a teenager in the 1980s, and from my journal entries during a first trip to China last May.

One of the only nonfiction books that I read more than once as a teenager was Ekaterina Jung's memoir, *Growing Up in Moscow*, an emigrant's recollection of her childhood in the USSR. I had particularly looked forward to Chapter 9, "Sex and the Soviet Teenager," which turned out to have much more to do with what wasn't allowed than what was: "One of the not-so-bad consequences of film censorship was that many teenagers turned to books, including classics, as the only available repository of smutty material." In spite of being born in New York City in the mid-1970s, to Dr. Spock–reading parents, I also learned most of what I knew about sex at that time from novels. (What teenager wants to talk to her parents about sex, particularly the kind of parents who *want* to talk about it?) I would occasionally choose something from the bookstore because the title or cover, without being obvious, seemed to promise some instruction. This method was inconsistent at best: Stephen Crane's *Maggie: A Girl of the Streets* was completely inscrutable, and Jean Auel's *Clan of the Cave Bear* trilogy, which my mother unwittingly bought for me— with the idea that it would encourage an interest in evolutionary biology—turned out to be shocking in its specificity.

As a teenager, Jung loved to read, was passionate about libraries, and hoped to be a writer, although her early efforts (romantic dramas involving political dissidents) ended in frustration. Her small insurrections—getting a fake ID in order to use the Foreign Language Library two years before it was permitted—were just my speed. She was a privileged young woman who experienced oppression in her own life in "one real way. . . . It wasn't just that I couldn't say what I believed—*I had to say things I didn't believe*, a distinction of no small consequence." Although Jung emphasized her relative advantages, and made light of the trials she endured before her family's emigration in 1980, to me she had all the nobility of the dissidents she admired.

I got the opportunity to go to China through the U.S. State Department's Bureau of International Information Programs. According to their mission statement: "IIP designs, develops, and implements a variety of information initiatives and strategic communications programs" for "key international audiences." A representative from the program told me that they had thought of me because some of the stories in my book *Lucky Girls* take place in Asia, and because the IIP wanted to start sending younger writers abroad. One State Department employee in China later suggested that these days the program was focusing on younger audiences, who had presumably become "key international audiences" in the fight against terrorism. Perhaps the thought was that younger writers would be better able to strategically communicate with these younger audiences—to make a good impression in not-so-virgin territory.

The plan was for me to meet with university students in five Chinese cities (Beijing, Tianjin, Guilin, Kunming, and Shanghai) to talk about writing and contemporary fiction. I had been studying Mandarin for two years, but I was counting on the Chinese university students I met to speak English; if we relied on my Chinese, we would be limited to such topics as "Shopping" and "At the Beijing Post Office." Nevertheless, in the weeks before my trip, I practiced phrases on anyone who would listen:

"Zhe tiao huang kuzi tai xiao le. Neng bu neng huan yi tiao?"

"What does that mean?" my sister asked patiently.

"This pair of yellow pants is too small. Can I exchange them?"

"Small yellow pants," my sister said. "You're all set."

Somehow, when I agreed to participate in the IIP program, I had pictured a version of my book tour. I imagined myself giving readings at the Chinese equivalent of small independent bookstores in the Pacific Northwest—not an analogy that makes much sense as it turns out. I managed not to consider the ominous prospect of an audience who would be listening in their second or third language. (It is my experience that relatively few people want to listen to fiction readings by first-time short story writers, even in their first language.) As soon as I arrived in China, I received e-mails from press officers in Beijing and Shanghai with the unsettling information that my "presentations" would each be two hours long. The e-mail from Beijing also informed me that my presentation in Tianjin (a satellite city about an hour by car from Beijing) would be preceded by an interview with Tianjin TV. The station had provided sample questions in advance:

1. Please tell us about your life, especially your life in Asia.
2. Which famous American writers have influenced you? (The most famous American writer in China is Hemingway.)
3. Give us your opinion on American contemporary literature and Asian culture, including Chinese culture.

The press officer concluded with a kind warning: "This interview will be unlike any you may have done in the past . . . or hopefully ever will do again."

The interviewer, a woman about my age, was wearing a futuristic white and silver jumpsuit, paired with high-heeled silver ankle boots. The idea was that she would ask her questions in Chinese, while I nodded and smiled; then a translator would convey the question to me in English, which I would answer while the interviewer nodded and smiled. They allowed me to pass on question number three (a bit daunting in scope); more important than what I said, the producer emphasized, was that I pretend the translator didn't exist—something I failed at so miserably that the translator had to switch seats, so that she was out of my line of sight.

Afterward I attempted to practice my Chinese, saying something that could be roughly translated as: "Thank you, thank you! Beautiful university! Very happy to come to China! Extremely happy to meet you!"

"Oh, you speak Chinese!" the producer said generously— after taking a moment to confirm that the sounds coming out of my mouth were indeed intended to approximate his language.

In Shanghai, the consular press officer had decided that we should distribute a story from my book in advance so that the students would be familiar with it. He told me he'd chosen "The Tutor," a story about an American teenaged girl living in Bombay and her Indian SAT tutor, for two reasons. First, the students I would be speaking to "tended to come from backgrounds where they had tutors, and they understand the tutor/pupil relationship—although in your story it departs from the norm, of course." (In my story, the pupil seduces the tutor, of course.) "Second, and this is more difficult to explain, we had to submit a story to the classes that took into account what the Chinese authorities would be willing to allow." Although all of my stories had "very real-life adult situations, including sexual situations," in "The Tutor," they were "handled in a subtle enough way that we could stay under the radar, as it were."

In spite of my nervousness, I was excited; the phrase, "under the radar," reminded me of *Growing Up in Moscow*. Although I don't think I admitted this to myself, part of the reason that I was interested in going to China—in fact, that I had started studying Chinese in the first place—was the exotic romance of a closed society, a place that kept secrets. As pathetic as this sounds, I wanted to know what it was like *not* to be free. How else could "freedom" mean anything at all?

2.

Budapest July 11, 1962: Forgot to observe yesterday that the people's sad faces were apparent even in the park where they were necking on the benches. The only time they would smile a little was on the dance floor of the hotel, with the band playing from American editions of "Artistry in Rhythm," "Saints," and a garbled version of "Peter Gunn." . . . Mummy was disturbed by the little children marching along like soldiers outside the Parliament building and the red-neckerchiefed "pioneers" who stared coldly at us as we passed them in a church we were visiting. [Our guide] either didn't understand or didn't answer when we asked if there were any comparable movements for parents who didn't want their children indoctrinated with communism.

I had been asked to talk about writing and publishing in America; the question I most wanted to ask the students I met, however, was whether they thought it made sense to write fiction from a point of view significantly different from your own. I talked about men writing as women, women writing as men, young people writing as old people and vice versa; but what I really wanted to know was whether they thought writers could exchange their identity (cultural, national, racial) for another. Wasn't there something wrong with that?

The prevailing wisdom, in my college literary theory workshops, was that there was something very wrong with it. The professor of my introductory literature seminar was of Native American descent; as we sat in class discussing Leslie Marmon Silko's "Ceremony," I remember realizing with horror that in my room at home was a picture of me one Halloween dressed as an Indian (the sort of Indian who was once called a "red Indian") wearing a blanket, a feather, holding my palm up next to my face: "How." What if my professor had seen that? What would he think if he knew about the "Indian Princesses," a version of the Boy Scouts in which little girls went on camping trips, sang Iroquois songs, and made traditional kachina dolls out of paint, feathers, and cardboard paper towel rolls— of which my father had unfortunately served as "Big Chief," in a headdress with feathers down to his ankles?

Like my classmates, I was soon letting words like *postcolonialism* and *essentialism* roll off my tongue as if they were natural to me—the same way I smoked my first joint and slept with my first college boyfriend. Essentialism—the idea that all human beings are at bottom similar, have similar needs and wants—was a relic by the time I got to college. The fuzzy seventies-style identity politics I had learned from my parents, that "underneath," people were all the same, was now taboo. Now people were *not* the same. As I progressed through my English major, I found myself taking classes from professors whose critical agenda was "new critic" or "poststructuralist," rather than "postcolonial" or "new historicist." I felt more comfortable talking about Andrew Marvell's metaphorical use of gardens, or enjambment in Robert Browning, than I did about such delicate subjects as race and nationality.

It seems to me now that essentialism is the thing that makes me a writer and, more important, a reader: the moment in fiction—I think of George Eliot and Alice Munro in particular—when the reader thinks, *Yes—that is exactly how I felt, and this is the first time I've ever seen it written down before.* Perhaps I hardly wrote in college because I had always imagined that when I did, I would sound somehow different from the way I sounded in real life. I expected to be stranger, more mysterious, and more complicated, like the writers I admired—Cormac McCarthy, William Gaddis, William Gass. Naturally, I was disgusted with what I first produced: realistic stories about girls growing up in families like mine. In my first fiction-writing classes, I solved the problem by cloaking these narratives in great clouds of mystifying language. No one would be able to accuse me of being ordinary or boring because no one, least of all myself, would be able to tell what I meant.

The first time I wrote honestly about an experience significantly different from my own was in the story the State Department approved for distribution to the students in Shanghai. I hadn't felt that there was anything wrong with choosing to write from that perspective—a young Indian man who'd grown up in Bombay—any more than I had in another story, from the point of view of an American man my father's age who had fought in Vietnam. I wrote about these characters because of what they had in common with me—both were writers—and didn't bother too much about what was different. But afterward I wondered: Can a young person write as an older person? Can a woman write as a man? Can a Chinese author take on an American perspective, and if so, can an American write from a Chinese point of view?

I finally had this question answered for me in Kunming, the capital of the pleasant southern province Yunnan, where the teachers warned me that the students would "not be like the ones in Beijing and Tianjin." "Speak more slowly," they instructed. "Don't read from your book—just tell them what the stories are about." In the late morning, about sixty students filed into a large, open classroom with tiers of wooden seats. I stood behind a podium, in front of a sign welcoming me (author of "Luky Girls") to Kunming. After my talk, as the students were filing out, a young man passed me a note.

"Not from me," he whispered, and disappeared:

To Nell,

I'm sorry that I was mind-absent sometimes during your talk, so I missed much. It's strange that I think Emily Dickson must be a lady like the very girl standing on the platform, shy, sensitive and intelligent.

You said you are hesitate when asked what you do. Well, ask yourself do you really like writing? Do you enjoy yourself in that process? Emily left us her best poems even after withdrew from social communication. A poet is a poet as long as she is writing poems, why bother to definite yourself? Write as long as you feel like.

Sincerely yours,
Renée

The comparison to Emily Dickinson is charming—it's true that I am female, Caucasian, and not a particularly avid partygoer—but unfortunately belongs to a gentle Chinese tradition of prefacing criticism with excessive praise. I had designed this talk for students at my own high school, whose primary anxieties were about how the choices they made now would affect their futures. Certainly there are many students in China who are consumed by exactly these worries. But there are also young people all over the world, like "Renée," who are prematurely wise. My talk was about the "choices" I had made in relation to writing; I forgot that you don't make choices when you're writing. You can write in a way that's unnatural to you, but you can't do it for very long. Sooner or later you find yourself writing as yourself, no matter how different that self ends up looking on the page. From childhood I remember English teachers talking about the importance of creativity, of "expressing yourself," but you don't write in order to express yourself. (That happens naturally, whether you like it or not.) You write because you feel like talking to someone; as soon as you no longer have anything to communicate, presumably you stop writing. You "write as long as you feel like."

In all of the classrooms I visited, there were certain questions that inevitably got asked. Some of these were the type of thing I might have asked a foreign writer in America; we're always curious to know what an outsider thinks of us—where we live, and our particular cultural obsessions:

"What is your impression of Guilin?"

"What are your views on Hemingway, Emily Dickinson, and Mark Twain?"

And:

"I see you have taken some inspiration in India and Thailand. Would you like to come and take some inspiration in China?"

When I told this student that I was hoping to come back to China, she looked at the ceiling for a moment, and remarked, "Then . . . I hope your next book isn't called *Depressed Girls*."

Other questions were practical, about life in America and Americans. Because the English teachers at each university were often at a loss as to how to introduce a fiction writer who had published only one book and won no international prizes, their introductions often fell back on the fact that I had graduated from Harvard. (Like Ernest Hemingway, Emily Dickinson, and Mark Twain, Harvard University enjoys widespread name recognition in China. A book called *Harvard Girl*, a mother's recollection of everything she did during her daughter's childhood to ensure that the girl would eventually go abroad to study there, has sold 1.5 million copies.) By the time I'd done three or four presentations, I was sick of answering questions about Harvard.

"Describe Harvard," one bored-looking male student in Kunming asked, as soon as I finished my talk.

"What specifically are you interested in?"

He looked at me as if he were talking to a small child. "How to apply there," he said.

In Shanghai, at a university that had been described to me as the "Yale of China," an extremely well-spoken student, who spiked his speech with "ums" and "you knows"—not in the lazy way of native English speakers, but as a kind of colloquial flourish—ventured a more abstract question: "In New York City, um, you know, if there is a Chinese boy? And he is very handsome and very smart, and also very rich? And an American girl is, um, you know, in love with him. Well, my question is, will she tell him that she loves him—or will she . . . "

His question, which had the entire class more attentive than they'd been until this point, was interrupted by a teacher in the front row, who stood up and preempted it: "Describe Harvard

University for our students, please, and give us your opinion on how it compares to the ancient universities of Europe."

So much for cultural exchange.

Even when the students were allowed to ask whatever they wanted, I often misunderstood the questions. At Nankai University in Tianjin, a female student raised her hand and asked whether it was important to have "heroes" in fiction. I spent some time talking about what I had learned from writing and literature teachers, and also from reading writers I admire. Reading, I told the student, was the only real way to learn to write.

"Does that answer your question?" I asked.

The student smiled and shook her head. "I mean, can a character in a story do bad things? Crimes or drugs or . . . other things? Or should the writer not put those things in stories, in case some reader might imitate them?"

This much more interesting question, which seemed to touch on the idea of censorship while phrasing it as a question about a writer's responsibility to her readers, was impressive, but I was struck even more by the student's willingness to correct me. At every Chinese university I visited, the desire to communicate on both sides was stronger than our shyness; of course, no communication is possible if we're too timid to tell each other when we've been misunderstood.

In Kunming I had lunch with an especially engaging young teacher, who had just come from teaching a class on "business English."

"Our textbook says Americans don't care about families," he told me apologetically. "They use the high divorce rate as evidence. But I don't think that's right?"

"That doesn't seem quite right," I agreed.

"Chinese writers don't know about America," he concluded with satisfaction.

"Most American writers don't know about China," I quickly countered, but the teacher was hardly interested in this banality. When I answered questions in China, I was careful to be safe. I wasn't worried about "what the Chinese authorities would allow"—as soon as I got to China I could see that for a foreigner, almost everything is allowed—but I had the common traveler's anxiety about making a cultural mistake and offending one's hosts. My answers to people's questions were often formulaic, and I found that they answered mine in the same way. Inevitably, the real opportunities came in listening to each other's questions rather than getting the answers.

After lunch, I went to the student bookstore, where I looked for and couldn't find the "business English" textbook. Instead I bought a book called *Colloquial English*, which, like my Chinese textbook, is made up of dialogues, reading-comprehension questions, and grammar exercises. Unlike my Chinese textbook, the book is focused in particular on colloquial language, designed to help students speak like real Americans—Americans such as "Batty" and "Harry," who show up in dialogues throughout the book:

BATTY: Tell me, Harry. Do you think Jenny has been playing a game? I have a hunch that she is trying to get closer to Mark.

HARRY: It's very clever of you. Now you see a better picture of the game. Mark has been on the gravy train. He's rolling in money these days.

BATTY: But Mark never goes steady with any girl. He may also be playing the field with Jenny.

HARRY: But Jenny is not the one who can be fooled. Mark will be outfoxed, I bet.

Colloquial English is precious to me—more precious than the scroll painting of a water buffalo I received as a thank you present in Tianjin, or the "Beijing Normal University" fountain pen, or the Miao minority embroidered purse from Yunnan University. It has the appeal of the children's party game telephone, the unbelievable slipperiness of language. "To have another thing coming," becomes "to have another think coming," and is translated into Chinese as *da cuo te cuo*, which my Chinese teacher roughly translates back: "big mistake, especially mistake." The book represents how far we're going to have to go in my lifetime, in order to understand both the dangers and the spectacular possibilities of the glib media word *globalization*. I'm not sure whether two people asking each other "Do citizens of your country care about their families?" qualifies as "strategic communication;" on the other hand, it feels like a place to start. Sometimes it seems like a miracle that we can understand each other at all.

3.

When my grandparents took my father to Eastern Europe in 1962, they drove a black Mercedes that they had rented in Munich.

"But a Mercedes there was just like a Ford here," my ninety-seven-year-old grandmother reminded me, when I asked her what she remembered about the trip. The frugal middle-class habits of the Freudenbergers are one of my grandmother's pre-occupations, along with our refined southern heritage. (The reality is almost exactly the opposite: No one in the family is particularly frugal, and according to my late great-uncle Rob, an amateur genealogist, the Freudenbergers come from a long line of "horse thieves and Tennessee dirt farmers.")

On the road from Skopie to Titograd, the car broke down. My father and his father, whom he called Joe, went to the state tourist office, leaving Mummy and the Ford-like Mercedes "in a peasant's front yard."

"She offered me some native wine," my grandmother told me. "Of course I declined." (My grandmother is a strict Baptist, proud of the fact that she's never tasted even communion wine; in her church, they substitute grape juice.) "I couldn't speak to her, but I rubbed my stomach to let her know. She understood me too!"

My grandmother remembered every detail of that breakdown: the gasoline coupons necessary for the tow truck and the names of passengers picked up along the way—a French family visiting relatives in Romania, who lent them small change and then refused to be reimbursed. The amount of space my father devoted to the breakdown in his journal suggests that for him, too, it was one of the most memorable events of the trip. He recalled Mr. Christian's description of their "miserable" relatives in Romania: "The tourist who goes behind the Iron Curtain, and does not have relatives to visit, doesn't see the bad side of communism." My father disagreed—the only time in the journal that he broke intellectual company with the adults around him:

One of Christian's brothers in Rumania confided in him that eventually, he feels, the satellite countries will get a chance to defect to the west, that the people are miserable under the commies.

They don't seem miserable in the countries we've seen. The commies seem to have raised the living standards and have certainly got rid of the royalty—which is good. But the lack of initiative the people show, how they seem unable to advance except through party channels, and the necessity of governing the people's republic through police-state measures seem to be the worst aspects of com'm.

What is the thing that sends us halfway around the world, makes us risk bad roads and unfamiliar food, not to mention sad faces and cold stares? Is it the desire to communicate? What makes communication across language and cultural barriers so thrilling, particularly to a family like ours—a family that, whatever else it might be, is full of awkward, shy people who are perhaps happier writing down their experiences than they were while they were having them?

We travel in order to cultivate ambivalence. Because we will never know what it's like to be someone else—our fathers, our neighbors, a farmer halfway across the world— doesn't mean that we shouldn't imagine and fail. Each act of imagination gives us, if not another experience, then another window on our own. It makes us sit up straighter, smooth our hair, think a moment before we open our mouths. On the bad road from Skopie to Titograd, my father and his parents had one of those sudden realizations common among travelers, and became aware of the eyes around them:

> The Germans are said not to be well-liked here, although we have seen no open signs of it. Since our car is German, we brought a small American flag, which we stuck up on the back ledge with chewing gum.

THE McEGGERS TANG CLAN

Robert Lanham

I love you, David Eggers. I want to run my fingers through your curly locks and draw your lips close to mine. I want to kiss your soft, silky mouth (oh I know it is) and consummate my love for you on a mattress filled with luxurious pages torn from The Believer, McSweeney's, A Heartbreaking Work of Staggering Genius, The Future Dictionary of America, You Shall Know Our Velocity, *and* Might. *If you feel timid, we can take things slowly. We could just spoon.* *

—ROBERT LANHAM

---

*The first rule of being a *McSweeney's* writer is to defy literary conventions. In this case, I have broken with convention by quoting myself in the prelude. In doing so, I evoke a response from the reader that makes him/her think, *Now there's something I ain't seen before. He sure must be book-smart.*

Part 1: Backlash is the Sound of Mimicry

Where the author addresses the reader and gets something pressing and emotionally charged off his chest:

Backlash against the backlash. Turn a deaf ear to the kids. Run to the closest independent bookstore in your neighborhood and consume. Bring some friends and encourage them to do the same.

Embrace our literary prince. You know you want to. Love him. Read him. Buy things from him. Buy more things from the people he knows. Shout his name from kingdom high. David! You complete me.

I appreciate you, David Eggers. I do. Indie rock is so twentieth-century. Indie publishing is the future. Criticizing you, I predict, will become passé. That issue you did on comics ruled.

Your critics are jealous. After all, you are the only person from our generation to create a bona fide literary movement. McSweeneyism.

Your entrepreneurship is groundbreaking. You give spreadsheets the finger. You rip bad art design a new asshole. You tear cheap paper stock to shreds. You are literature's MTV. Publishing's IFC. You are the RZA. *McSweeney's* is your Wu-Tang. Pay the McSweeney-phobes no heed, Mr. Eggers. Mofos can't keep a good nigga down.

You should be an inspiration. You defy the boomers' pillaging of our time in the spotlight. They called us slackers. They only allotted us a few measly years before changing our label to Generation Y. Before they clock us out completely and introduce Generation Z, let us reclaim, together, what has been taken. You have never been shy. This is Generation Eggers.

 Part 2: The End of the Age of Fair Vanity

Where the author defines backlash, discusses Graydon Carter, David Eggers, and Felicity reruns, while defying his urge to comment on how tomatoes should never be stir-fried.

backlash –n– To have an antagonistic reaction to an event or trend

***McSweeney's* backlash** –n– To have an antagonistic reaction toward *McSweeney's*, generally associated with people who subscribe religiously to *McSweeney's* publications, have an ironic sensibility, and realize when something has become passé well before *you* ever could.

No one felt the blow of Graydon Carter's statement "It's the end of the age of irony" harder than David Eggers.* After

---

Vanity Fair editor Graydon Carter was a founder of *Spy*, a direct competitor of Eggers's *Might Magazine*. Many have suggested Carter's assertion that irony is dead was an attempt to undermine rival editor David Eggers's career and thus prove that earnest celebrity interviews with Tom Cruise are more literary than sarcastic, self-reflexive short stories and experimental criticism. Actually, disregard this rubbish. I just wanted to add some superfluous footnoting to illustrate how it's done.

all, *McSweeney's* irony has always been his bread and butter. In the fallout, legions of Eggers's fans turned their backs on him. He became the whipping boy of contemporary lit, not to mention the scapegoated poster boy of the ironic aesthetic. People have written Eggers off for years, meanwhile mimicking his style, buying books published under the *McSweeney's* moniker, and renewing their subscriptions to his publications.

In an apparent attempt to repackage himself, Eggers began publishing *The Believer,* a monthly literary magazine with a slightly less ironic sensibility.* Just as Fox News is "fair and balanced," *The Believer* is snark-free and insightful. It even has a section on its Web site called "The Snarkwatch," which keeps literary cynicism in check by exposing and printing unfair critical jabs taken at authors. "Snarkwatch" is like problem solvers on the network news, only for elite, insular, well-connected Ivy League English majors who have been wrongly misrepresented by The Man. Want to publish an essay that consists solely of acknowledgments and an ink drawing of a praying mantis? Worry not about mindless critics attacking your artistry. Snarkwatch has arrived.

---

*Though Heidi Julavits is the official editor of *The Believer,* Eggers's fingerprints are all over the publication, and if you breathe deeply while reading, you may even catch a whiff of his English Leather cologne coming from its pages. (Reportedly, he sometimes wears Chaps.) Eggers recently compiled *The Future Dictionary of America,* coscripted a play, and continues to publish books by other *McSweeney's* authors while being fed grapes by lifelike androids with breasts that are "just the right size."

Though experimental at times, Eggers thankfully has the wisdom to know when a tried-and-true formula should not be tampered with. He will keep his trademark curly locks fashionably longish.

"I learned a lot from watching reruns of Felicity," *Eggers claims. "I still can't believe she cut it [her hair] so short."*

But what is McSweeneyism, anyway? Is it a writing style? Is it an elite social club? Is there a handshake? Are there colors that should be worn like the Bloods' and the Crips'? Are there keggers with pizza, drunk sorority chicks, and guys in baseball caps? Will there be trading cards featuring the faces of Aimee Bender, Rick Moody, Colson Whitehead, George Saunders, John Hodgman, and Zadie Smith? Is McSweeneyism a cultural movement on a par with magic realism, modernism, or the industrial revolution?

Many of these questions remain cloaked in mystery. Like the Masons and Skull & Bones, the members of the *McSweeney's* clan have all taken an oath of silence. Even the *McSweeney's* logo rings cryptic: "Made with only you in mind by people you do not know."

The only way to unlock their secrets is to become a *McSweeney's* writer yourself. And I'm about to tell you how.*

---

*In addition to countless hours studying *McSweeney's* texts, the secrets unveiled in this study are a result of undercover research by *Blue Lagoon's* Christopher Atkins. A dead ringer for Eggers after dying his hair brown, Atkins posed as Eggers and successfully infiltrated the secret *McSweeney's* lair to help us conduct our study.

Part 3: A Brief Interlude

Where the author diverges for a moment to list general rules that all writers should follow, McSweeney's writers and otherwise.*

Rule number one: Embrace poverty. After all, *author* is a glorified way of saying "works two jobs." (Note: *Author* sometimes means "inherited money" or "lives in sister-in-law's tool shed on a permanent diet of rice and soy sauce.")

Rule number two: Poetry is for college students and people who are too lazy to write prose. If you *must* write poetry, refrain from using old English spellings and words like *candelabra* (unless you're Wiccan).

Rule number three: Do not allow yourself to be distracted by the three sirens of literature:

1. Writing groups. They are simply a way to procrastinate.
2. Graduate school. See *Writing groups*.
3. McGriddle breakfast sandwiches.

Rule number four: Like chronic masturbation, checking your Amazon rank too frequently can cause blindness and impotence.

Rule number five: Never criticize Barnes and Noble. Their reps are often consulted before publishing houses make their final bids on a book. Plus, they've been known to send Paolo

---

*Though this list of rules is intended for anyone who wants to be a writer, tangential interludes (such as the one above) are recommended *specifically* for the *McSweeney's* writer.

and Joey over to rough up unruly authors. Save a bit of your advance to bribe the smarmy dude with psoriasis who works the Staff Recommendations table.

Rule number six: Never refer to Shakespeare as "the Bard."

Rule number seven: Most writers submit their work through an agent. We suggest choosing one with a strong industry nickname like The Jackal. On the other hand, one should avoid an agent who has a nickname like The Leprechaun, Dough Boy, or Milky.

Agent Nicknames Part 1:

Good Nicknames	*Bad Nicknames*
The Wolf	The Ferret
Poker Face	Dickhead
The Magic	The Wiccan
Sledgehammer	Lug Nut
The Shark	The Tick-Infested Lamb
The General	The Albino
The Axe	The Tool
The Insider	The Leper
Ironside	Felt Tip
The Mayor	Falco
Wonder Woman	Monkey Man
Five Star	Peanut, Butter, and Jelly
Mr. Up-Sell	Mumbles

 Part 4: The Nitty-Gritty

Where the author and a team of trained McSweeney's *scholars discuss how to become a* McSweeney's *writer and, if there's time, robots.*

Living the Life: Creating a *McSweeney's* Persona

Becoming a genuine *McSweeney's* writer requires devotion. Being original on the written page is rarely enough. You need to shape an appropriate persona for yourself off the page as well. The following are some key ways to stand out from the crowd:

A: *Create a Good Myth about Your Educational and Professional Background*
(It is OK to take poetic license on your background and cred. You are a writer after all.)

Choose one of the following:

Prestigious bio: 1. Stuyvesant High School/MFA in English from University of Iowa/articles published in the *New Yorker* and *Harper's*

Well-rounded bio: 2. Catholic high school/B.A. from Stanford/articles published in the *New Yorker* and *Harper's*

Ironic bio: 3. High school dropout/short stint smuggling Mexicans across the border/articles published in the *New Yorker* and *Harper's*

B: *Pick a Strong Muse*

Since people will always ask who your influences are, choose an original writer to emulate. Thomas Berger or Harry Crews are safe choices. They are literary. They are established. And no one on the planet Earth has ever heard of them. Claiming that one of the aforementioned is an influence can immediately make you sound smart. Dickens is another good example, since he has long been out of favor due to overexposure in junior high school. Plus, plot-heavy writers from previous generations are *en vogue* at McSweeney's these days. Sarcastic choices like Danielle Steele and Nora Roberts can be equally rewarding.

C: *Walk the Walk, Talk the Talk*
1. Attend readings by other McSweeney's authors in your area.
2. Add some flair by accessorizing with an ironic "I hate literature" button, or better yet, get a tattoo that says "working-class hero."
3. When people ask you what you do for a living, say you are writing a memoir.
4. Openly criticize Barnes and Noble within earshot of others (unless you are doing a reading there).
5. Coopt a portion of a popular McSweeney's writer's name to confuse others into noticing you. For example, Robert Lanham could become Robert Safran Lanham or Robert Foster Lanham.

D: *Create an Ironic Phrase for the Last Sentence of Your Author's Bio*
Sample: "*Insert Name* lives and works in Wicker Park, Chicago, and is saving up for a nice table saw."

Know Your Audience
(AKA they weren't popular in grade school and resent all things considered popular now)

McSweeney's writers should never attempt to be popular or appeal to a wide audience. Instead, write to impress English majors and other authors. After all, only they are smart enough to appreciate that special thing you do. Impressing other writers helps ensure that they will whisper sweet nothings about you to their agents and their editors.

Is Plot a Four-Letter Word?

Plot is not necessarily a bad word to the typical McSweeney's writer; there are just easier and more creative ways to spin a yarn. Relying on plot to tell a story is a crutch.* Who needs exhaustive plot as long as your characters are quirky? In general, plot-driven writing is respectable only if it comes from another era. Exceptions are sometimes made for eccentric comedy writers who appear on NPR and authors who have the first name Jonathan.

Occasionally, McSweeney's will make a concession and devote an issue to plot, provided the narrative references a kitschy genre like forties detective novels or Victorian romance serials. In this context, authors can have fun, without sacrificing academic shrewdness, since they are referencing another literary era. And since kitsch is the heartbeat of McSweeneyism, lots of cool retro art can be featured when authors affectionately allude to other eras. Finding an opportunity to include dime-novel-style art, reportedly, leaves David "all tingly" with excitement.

---

*Despite his popularity and plot-driven style, Stephen King is now quietly embraced by the McSweeney's literati, since he was embraced by the New York Times as a modern-day Dickens. He is an exception to the "plot is to be avoided" rule.

Choosing a Tone

Whether writing a book review, a short story, or a comedic list about the people who made fun of you in high school, the *McSweeney's* writer should pick a tone that he/she feels most comfortable with. Here are the most popular choices:

Circle one:
academically clever
snarky clever
playfully adorably clever
self-indulgent
NPR-ready
self-effacing
refreshingly sincere

The Perfect Title

Your title does not necessarily need to reflect the content of your piece, but a strong *McSweeney's* title should catch its readers off guard with the right amount of absurdity and/or inaccessibility. Here are a few examples of strong titles:

1. Brahman by Birth, Literary Messiah by the Grace of an Ivy League
2. A Review of George Saunders by Someone Who Knows George Saunders
3. Pirates, Pirates, Parrots, Ferrets
4. Ten Phrases Uttered by My Mother Every Thanksgiving

5. A Meta Exegesis of Meta-Writer's-Block Literature with Footnotes by Me

6. The Contents of an Everyday Household Glass Cleaner

7. Another Rick Moody Review

8. Important Dispatch: I Can Never Get Enough Nougat

9. Things I Found in My Pocket after Passing Out at a Blue Oyster Cult Reunion Concert That I Didn't Attend Ironically

10. An Essay by a Woman. You Know, to Fill That 15 Percent Quota

11. People Don't Understand the True Me When They Say I'm Self-Indulgent

12. One More Rick Moody Review

 The Body of Your Piece

When writing for an Eggers publication, the main rule of thumb is to be original at all costs. *McSweeney's* was founded on the principle that literature should take chances and not follow a doctrine. The invented mascot, Timothy McSweeney, after all is described as being "a troubled fellow, an outsider, a probable genius of indeterminate age [who] wanted attention, some consideration, an attentive ear."

On a more concrete level, anyone familiar with *McSweeney's* knows that a good short story contains rich character development, a vivid sense of time and place, and a retro diagram, or medical drawing. When writing a nonfiction essay or review, be sure to include a pie chart or a graph. If you feel stuck and simply cannot come up with an idea, dig that rejection letter out of the waste basket and type it up verbatim. Don't have a rejection letter? The electric bill will work just as well!

Another surefire way to impress the *McSweeney's* masthead is to appear neurotic. We recommend coming up with a concept that requires obsessive research but promises no meaningful reward. For instance, fleshing out a piece that catalogs the number of sports metaphors used in non-sports sections of the *Boston Herald* in 2004 is an excellent concept for a *McSweeney's* essay. If you author a quirky piece such as this, people will automatically assume you are neurotic, a trait that is on a par with talent and/or an Ivy League education. After all, that "troubled fellow" Timothy McSweeney is always on the hunt for more troubled fellows.

And do not be afraid to experiment. If your piece sucks, you can always tinker with the design or insert an ink drawing of a lawnmower to distract people from noticing.

Agent Nicknames Part 2:

Good Nicknames	*Bad Nicknames*
The Negotiator	Dial Tone
The Chairman	The Goblin
Slim Shady	Nickels
Queen Liz	Cherry
Big Stick	Whiskers
Speedy	Captain Pancake
The Bear	The Gummy Bear
M-16	Skeeter
Uptown-Downtown	
Murphy Brown	Gidget
Vader	The Wookiee

The Enforcer	Swamp Dawg
Mr. Deal	Cheese Puff Carol
Mr. Charisma	Ipecac

Bells and Whistles

Those desiring to adhere to true *McSweeney's* style should in-clude plenty of bells, whistles, and typographical gimmicks. Often these little extras can be more important than the con-tent itself. In fact, an experienced *McSweeney's* writer can even create an entire piece *just from the bells and whistles*. To be au-thentic, we recommend doing at least one of the following:

a. Discuss at length your fondness for the Arial Adelphi font in point size 10.
b. Write in the form of an instant message correspondence.
c. Put a majority of your content in footnotes.
d. Have your mom add margin notes critiquing your writ-ing, and incorporate them into your piece.
e. Include a fake blurb by Oprah.
f. Provide a "rules and suggestions for reading" sidebar.
g. Add a Victorian-style summary as a prelude.
h. Using a mirror, stare at yourself seductively with puck-ered lips for thirty minutes daily.

Note: If you cannot find a place for any of the above, have an artistic friend sketch out a bell and a whistle and insert them at will throughout your piece with the respective captions "Bell" and "Whistle."

Sending Your Submission to a *McSweeney's* Publication

Even an unorthodox institution like *McSweeney's* expects a certain degree of professionalism when it comes to submissions. We recommend including a cover letter (preferably on an agent's letterhead) that compares your writing style to other *McSweeney's* authors'. Saying your writing style is *Zadie Smith meets Colson Whitehead with a touch of Aimee Bender* is a good solid choice.

Before sending a submission, write a short synopsis of your piece using the *McSweeney's* format. After all, even the altruistic staff at *McSweeney's* are pressed for time in this busy day and age. Here's a sample of correct and incorrect ways to write a *McSweeney's* synopsis.

The incorrect way: The attached story is a comedic account of my life growing up next door to an elusive neighbor who may or may not be J. D. Salinger.

The correct way: The attached story is a comedic account of my life growing up next door to an elusive neighbor who may or may not be J. D. Salinger, where the truth about several of the following is discovered: baking-soda-enriched toothpaste, power tools, cuneiform tablet forgeries, chicken, and the value of good old-fashioned platonic friendship.

The Classic *McSweeney's* Ending

Since most writers find that coming up with a strong ending is the hardest part of the process, we've saved this lesson for last.

To ensure success, we recommend ending your piece in a classic *McSweeney's* style. Whether you're writing a short story or an essay, ending on a gimmick is always preferable to a concise finish where all the variables fall neatly into place. If you're at a loss, here are two sample styles to choose from:

Sample Ending 1: The Discussion Kitsch Style
Reader discussion questions:

1. True or False: Graydon Carter actually said, "Irony is gay."
2. Is the word *McSweeney's* the onomatopoeic sound of hipster self-loathing?
3. Are Vin Diesel and the Rock the same person?
4. Is it human nature to be the hardest on those who are also the most talented?

Sample Ending 2: The Facetious Cliffhanger Style
Check back next week when we'll be discussing:

1. The nonexistence and absurdity in concept of so-called lad lit.
2. How making your protagonist an executive and changing the setting to the Condé Nast building can transform your mundane chick lit novel into a hip chick lit novel.
3. The proper ingredients needed to make quail stew refreshing yet hearty.
4. That nice girl at Walgreens with the oily skin.

And Most Important . . .

If you get published by a *McSweeney's* publication, do not boast about it. Formally affiliating yourself with the McEggers Tang Clan would not be original! Deny it. Change the subject. Dismiss the *McSweeney's* phenomenon by saying, "That shit is so 2001." You needed the money. A résumé builder. Claim that *McSweeney's* is a trend, just like rap music.

After all, no one *really* writes quirky, self-reflexive pieces anymore. No one is ever snarky. No one has strayed from standard writing conventions in years. Literary movements don't happen anymore. Equal® and Splenda® taste better than sugar. And we can thank our lucky stars (and some say Eggers) that irony is truly, completely, categorically, unequivocally, and definitively dead.

121 YEARS OF SOLITUDE

Paul Collins

It began, as most things do, when I was busy reaching for something else. I'd noticed a Victorian children's annual in the back room of a book dealer's shop in Hereford; trying to grab it from atop a ceiling-high stack, I steadied myself on a bookshelf, where my hand fell upon a black volume in octavo: *Notes and Queries: A Medium of Intercommunication for Literary Men*, its subtitle promised. It was the bound volume of a weekly magazine of Victorian gentlemen writing in with any question or notion that came into their heads; fellow readers ventured to answer them in the following weeks. It was a coal-fired Friendster, a horse-and-buggy blog, with thousands of threads tangling into a glorious asynchronous mess.

One such query simply read:

"RATS DESERT A SINKING SHIP." Do they? And where do they go?
                    JOHN J. BARDWELL WORKARD, M.A.

Others unearthed random shards of history: "Puritan An-
tipathy to Custard," an article declared. "Job's Disease," another promised: Its writer was seeking an old banned medical
paper suggesting that Job's afflictions were symptomatic of
syphilis. Nearby, correspondents debated the old architectural
practice of planting a decapitated horse head under the flag-
stones of any newly built church or music hall; this was
thought to somehow improve a building's acoustics.

"What an odd book," I thought to myself. I bought it,
moved to another country, and thought no more of the matter
for a couple years.

• • •

The public library in Portland, Oregon, is marble and monu-
mental, a brooding thing—from an age when books got
housed in something halfway between a capitol rotunda and a
crypt. I'm a regular there, but a passing one. With a printout
from an online catalog in hand, I'm in and out in a few minutes. I don't know what possessed me one day to pause on my
way to out and tap three words into a catalog workstation:
"Notes . . . and . . . Queries."

The library had it. They had all of it. In fact, unknown to
me, the magazine was not some quirk of the mid-nineteenth
century. It was *still in print*, and had been continuously since
1848. Portland had an entire hardbound run of it—about two
hundred and fifty volumes. I did some quick multiplication:
150,000 pages, give or take. That was about 148,000 pages
longer than anything else I'd ever attempted to read.

What if?—I wondered. What if *I read the whole thing?*

The idea had a curious appeal to me. I tend to read four or five books at a time, zigzagging from one thing to the next; I don't think I'd been truly immersed in a series of books since tackling Asimov's *Foundation* quartet over one long weekend as a teenager. And reading 250 volumes of anything seemed insane, or at least insanely overwhelming. Still . . . two hundred and fifty. That was roughly the number of weekdays in an entire year. Maybe it was like climbing at a great height; I'd be OK as long as I didn't look down. I couldn't actually see the 250 volumes, after all: Most of them were kept in storage. Patrons of the library could only get them one volume at a time from a paging desk. And I could certainly read one book at a time . . . couldn't I?

So I developed a routine. Every afternoon I'd ride the bus downtown, reading the latest news as a prelude to reading last century's news. Then I'd grab up a cup of coffee to fortify myself, trudge up the grand staircase to the second floor, and procure my copy of *Notes and Queries* for the day. I came to recognize the editors, the correspondents, even the companies in the ads; I knew when they retired, went bankrupt, died. I watched the beloved first editor hand over the reins, and read his obituary soon afterward; I saw correspondent John Timbs ailing in 1874—"There is a man down in the battle of life. . . . A little help will enable Mr. Timbs to renew the struggle"—and watched pledges roll in from fellow antiquarians like Mr. Appleyard, Mr. Churchill, and mysterious pseudonymous correspondents. I am happy to report that one Mr. "Caw, As The Crow Sings" made a donation of one pound and one shilling.

Timbs died; his benefactors died, too. Each decade rolled by like the miles on an odometer: Reaching January 1900 was like crossing a state line. I felt like telling someone else in the library, but I couldn't; they'd simply have stared at me. I was not having the prescribed modern library experience; I was not reading the expensive new books or using the expensive new equipment. I had gone off the grid, electronically and typographically, into The Land That Timeliness Forgot. When you click into archived articles formatted into six-inch-wide printer-friendly blocks of 12-point text, you don't get the nervous jostling of multiple columns of tiny print; the eye can't leap from item to item. And half the page is always missing. I don't mean the text: I mean the *ads*. If you read an 1873 *Notes* ad for Gentleman's Porpoise Hide Boots—"very soft and very strong," if we are to believe Mr. Marshall of 192 Oxford Street—you are perhaps less liable to disbelieve other revelations of readers making whiskey from sawdust, church altars out of cheese, paintings on cobwebs ("The subject of mine is a very charming young woman"), or, for that matter, a *dress* made of cobwebs. Apparently the latter was presented to Queen Victoria by the Empress of Brazil in 1877.

Days, weeks, and then months passed. I learned where the best seats were. I insensibly made a slow figure 8 in my seat selections, for the periodical room's windows face west; with each month the slant of afternoon sun coming in changed. And I found the every day was like swimming under water: Each time I'd emerge at the end, blinking at the sunlight after feeling like I was about to burst, and looking back to find that I was far, far away from where I had dived in. Each day the dive got easier: I could submerge myself longer and deeper, until I almost felt as if I needn't come up for air at all if I didn't feel like it.

The thing is, every *Notes and Queries* led only to more books, to more notes and more queries: It was endlessly bibliographic. I had started with the intention of reading a couple hundred books; it is impossible not to end feeling the need to read a couple thousand more. And that didn't even include what I found in the "Books" column at the end of each issue, some of whose titles beggared belief. In 1873 we hear about *The Tongue Not Essential to Speech*, by the Honorable Edward Twisleton. It's a medical and historical treatise on people whose tongues have been ripped out. And guess what? It turns out how that . . . um, well, the tongue is not essential to speech. (It does, Twisleton noted, certainly *help* to have one.) Not to be outdone, in 1948 there appeared a review of Claude Messent's magnificently obscure *Old Door Knockers of Norwich*, a tome which opens with the indubitably true statement that "this is the first book ever to have been published entirely on the subject of Door Knockers." Even if it isn't, I think it's safe to say that neither you nor I nor anyone other than Claude Messent is likely to go to the trouble of finding out.

Well, we all have our random obsessions, and now I had mine. There were others there with me, library patrons who spent most of the afternoon, if not most of the day, in the building. I started to recognize them. There was the retired gentleman in tweed who came in each day to work on his genealogical searches, searching county death records before he became the newest entry. There were the homeless guys who snored quietly in the corners, the pretence of a magazine held in their laps. And then there were people who were simply always *there*, and always *reading*: the guy who wore sunglasses and ski hats in any weather; the buzz-cut teen smelling of Speed Stick who read car magazines; the old man who appeared to be a golem conjured from phlegm and uric acid; the muttering woman who appeared one day outside Periodicals with her belongings piled into a hijacked airport Smarte Carte, as if she expected to find the International Terminal somewhere between *Popular Mechanics* and *Prevention*.

None of us ever acknowledged each other's presence. We only acknowledged books, and I came to know mine well. The library bought much of its run from one man: His corrections and bibliographic notes, in old brown ink, are evident throughout. His is the spidery writing of the Victorian steel-nibbed pen, and my own notebook scribblings in ballpoint looked oafish next to it. But it felt reassuring to know that another man had walked this dark and forgotten path of reading. By the late 1870s, though, I noticed the writing getting shakier and less frequent until, one day, it stopped altogether. I flipped through an entire volume without finding his telltale calligraphy; the next volume was empty, too. I pulled my Walkman headphones off and sat there a moment. The volumes sat on my desk, mute, and I looked up from them, through the library windows, and at the clouds drifting by. I realized that my silent companion had died. And—absurdly, I know—I felt a little pang, even though I never knew his name, and he died a hundred years before I was born.

• • •

What struck me the most when immersed in *Notes and Queries*—in reading history itself—was this almost constant realization that we are *not* alone; that our paths have been trod before, by walkers who fell long before we ever arose. No one is more aware of this than *N&Q*'s own writers. The magazine's very existence is held up in one early issue as an apt reincarnation. "'There is nothing new under the sun,' quoth the Preacher; and the same must be said of *Notes and Queries*," reports a correspondent, who then notes that its format is identical to such long-forgotten newsletters as *Memoirs for the Ingenious* (1693), *Memoirs for the Curious* (1701), *the Athenian Oracle* (1704), *the Delphick Oracle* (1720), and the *British Apollo* (1740). That last title, he notes, includes the eternal I-dunno question: Why is yawning so infectious? The explanation in 1740 was that, well, because it *is* infectious:

> Gaping or yawning is infectious, because the steams of blood being ejected out of the mouth, both infect the ambient air, which being received by the nostrils into another man's mouth, doth irritate the fibres of the hypogastric muscle to open the mouth to discharge by expiration the unfortunate gust of air infected with the steams of blood, as aforesaid.

This, if maybe not the most believable explanation of yawning, still anticipates the transmission of *Ebola* pretty handily.

Other questions were equally baffling both then and now. In the December 3, 1910, issue, a reader asks:

SCISSORS AND JAWS. Some men when making a continued use of scissors move their jaws in sympathy, Is this at all common? Does it occur among women? And among such people as tailors and paper-hangers?

W.C.B.

The following issue was filled with responses: "Yes! Yes! Everyone *does* do that!" And so, too, do I—with staplers. I remember having to do so much stapling one night that my jaw hurt afterward, from the unconscious clenching of it with each compression of the Swingline. I have never found this physiological curiosity noted or explained anywhere else, before or since.

Sometimes the same questions appeared over and over again, every couple of decades, such as the query about whose old cookbook recipe began with the line "First, catch your hare." In early issues Victorian readers puzzled over the origins of a venerable patent medicine with the delightful name of Daffy's Elixir; in the 1950s, their great-grandchildren were still puzzling over it. And fashion cycles that seemed modern to me suddenly became less so: If you think the unfashionable ponytails you see on aging boomers is a modern phenomenon, take in this sentence: "I saw the other day descending from a carriage in Cheapside a venerable old gentleman with a little screw of his grey locks tied behind with a short riband, the expiring form of this once universal execresance." It was published in the October 30, 1858, issue. Or try this peek into the wardrobe: "I have seen a pair of high-heeled shoes that belonged to a female ancestor, who died about forty years ago, aged about ninety. . . . When were such shoes introduced into fashion? And when did the fashion cease? The shoes must have been uncommonly uncomfortable." These disco-ready metallic bronze-colored four-inch heels are not from Donna Summers's yard sale; the letter was published in 1860. Women marveling at these "uncommonly uncomfortable" old shoes were themselves liable to be wearing rib-crushing whalebone corsets.

We should appear equally ridiculous to our progeny: Most generations do. But it will not be as obvious to them, because the contradictions will be hidden. They will find their facts in the sensible way, in a database, singular expressions yanked from the context and crosstalk of pages of competing articles and advertising. There's no point in decrying or even mourning the loss: It is going to happen. They, like us, will simply tap in, print out, and leave.

But I stayed. I stayed, though I found the magazine increasingly intolerable after the 1940s; editors who have been dead for thirty years now received my daily wrath for having betrayed editors dead for 60, 100, 130 years. Why? Well, they let the academics take over. *Notes & Queries* had been a journal of learned men, but never professionally learned men. And now? Professors, dons, deans, institute denizens—and all them, at heart, lecturers. They had only Notes, never Queries. They were always holding forth on the trivial points of Great Works, instead of upon the great points of Trivial Works. In came the tropes of Milton, and Shakespeare, and Eliot; out went the retired bus drivers and eccentric accountants with their tales of men baking themselves in ovens on a bet, and beehives found inside skulls. But I kept reading until 1969, when the replacement of the books by microfilm was the final straw.

By the time I was born, it was all over for me.

Four seasons had passed outside; four hundred and eighty four inside. I had fallen through a trapdoor into a another time, another place. I cannot truly describe the experience except to say that it was like spending a year in another country, one where I spoke the language but did not know the first thing about its culture. I may even go back again someday.

LYING TO THE OPTICIAN: THE READING EXPERIENCE RATED

Tracy Chevalier

Over the years I've fielded many questions from journalists and readers about writing and reading. I don't mind; I'm a talker and like answering questions. But there is one question that makes me shudder, no matter how often I answer it or how hard I think about it: What are your Top Ten books? Sometimes the question has been framed differently: Which authors have influenced you the most? Or what are the ten books you would like always to have on your bedside table? Or—this from *Oprah Magazine*, with its relentless aspirational spin—name five books that have made a difference to your life. No matter how it's put, someone wants me to pronounce on my reading experiences and, presumably, reveal something of myself.

Lord, how I hate it. I hate it even though I've asked people the same question myself, have pondered others' lists, or their bookshelves, or what they're reading on the subway. I want to know what my friends have read on vacation. I think differently of someone who prefers Wilkie Collins over Charles Dickens, or Updike over Roth, or the *Chronicles of Narnia* over *Lord of the Rings*. It's a given that our choice of books reveals our personalities, so surely it's a legitimate question to ask writers, or anyone, what books they love. Yet I sweat over my list, worrying over it, changing it, doubting its veracity. It's the same feeling I get when I'm at the optician's having my eyes tested and she asks, "Which letter is clearer on the chart, the left E or the right E?" And I'm not sure because they look the same, but I have to choose because she needs a definite answer so that she can adjust my contact lenses. Whatever I answer, my choice feels so arbitrary that I wonder if I might be unintentionally lying.

I'm certainly familiar with the Top Ten format. I grew up listening to Casey Kasem every week, and I always look at the best seller lists when I read the books section of the newspaper or on Amazon. I thought the best parts of Nick Hornby's *High Fidelity* were the lists. And I don't mind being asked about my Top Ten films or albums. An Italian journalist once gave me five minutes to write down my five favorite films, albums, and books. I did the first two in a couple of minutes, but the books I stalled on and couldn't finish. I am more at ease talking about music and films because they're not my livelihood. Now that I am a writer by trade, I feel more responsible and less cavalier about my pronouncements on books. I'm expected to know better, not to be suckered by the literary equivalent of a mediocre Lyle Lovett album or the pretensions of *The Matrix* films. And I'm aware that my list is meant to be a projection of me, or at least of how I want people to see me. These factors make it hard not to be self-conscious about the list.

Casey Kasem and Amazon have it easy: Their lists are based on quantity, not quality. There is a simple, finite answer to what the Top Ten are on Amazon on October 1, 2004, at 11:30 A.M. (No. 1 is *Jon Stewart Presents America: A Citizen's Guide to Democracy Inaction*): It's how many have sold the most in the last hour. To come up with a Top Ten of all-time favorites is much trickier. It's meant to be more permanent and less questionable. Yet my own Top Ten are almost as changeable as Casey Kasem's, even though not linked to economics. At 11:30 A.M. on October 1, 2004, I am likely to include *Anna Karenina* as one of my Top Ten. On October 2, 2004, though, I might think it too long, too sentimental, too Oprah for my list.

Whenever I'm obliged to name my Top Ten I flounder between the Canon and the best sellers, the Big Books and the Best Loved, the head and the heart. This is not a new dilemma for me. On my own Web site I include a list of what I've read each month, with a star system of rating the books: one star for terrible, five stars for superb. For the first eighteen months I gave the books a single rating. After a while, though, I found the pressure to rate them was interfering with my reading experience. I could no longer enjoy a book, but fretted throughout as to whether to give it, say, three or four stars. I felt so compromised by having to rate the books that I considered dropping it, even though from feedback I knew that people loved seeing the ratings.

Finally I realized that I was usually torn between two conflicting ratings: one for whether or not the book was well written, the other for my reading experience of it. Perhaps—given how often the head and heart are at war—it's not surprising that these two ratings often don't match. Just because a book is well written doesn't mean we like reading it. Conversely, a book can be poorly written but entertaining, especially if it's just what we're in the mood for at the time. I decided to be honest, and now I give books two ratings: one for the quality of the book itself (its style, structure, originality, etc.), the other for whether or not I actually had a good time reading it.

I suspect the first rating will remain the same over time—after all, the book itself never changes—but the second one may shift. Inevitably, the feeling we have of reading a great book fades, as fireworks, flower scents, and love affairs do. After a while all we can rank is our memory of how we felt about it. It's a bit like recalling a vacation by looking at photo albums, which are only of "good" shots and don't necessarily tell the full story of the trip. With only those photos as prompts, our memories of the vacation become about the Kodak moments rather than the other 99 percent.

My memory of specific details in books is terrible. Often I can't remember how books end. What happens at the end of *The Catcher in the Rye*? Or Margaret Atwood's *Alias Grace*? Or Rose Tremain's *Restoration*? All have been in my Top Ten at one time or another. I remember loving some of Atwood's early novels, but that's all I remember. I read them at least twenty years ago; what would I think of them now? Is it legal to say you love a book when you can't actually remember anything about it? In fact, when I think of the books I was so passionate about when I was young, I wonder if I would love them as much now. When the films of *Lord of the Rings* came out, several friends admitted trying to reread the books they had loved as teenagers, but they couldn't finish them. Me, I'm preserving my teenage obsession.

Could the same also be said of books I read in early adulthood? Or ten years ago? Or even a year ago? In 2003 I read just one book I gave five stars to: Ann Patchett's *Bel Canto*. On looking over my ratings now, I noticed, too, that I gave Mark Haddon's *Curious Incident of the Dog in the Night-Time* just three stars. A year on, would I change either rating? Yes— I think they would both get four stars. Maybe next year those stars would be changed yet again. My response to a book is built on shifting sands, buffeted by the other books I read, the things other people say about the books, and how much the book continues to ring bells in my head or disappears among all the others.

It's not just our memory that is fickle—so are our reading experiences. The process of reading and absorbing a book is very much tied to the time and place and emotional state in which the books are read. Starting with L. M. Montgomery's *Anne of Green Gables* at age eleven and up through Philip Pullman's *His Dark Materials* in 2002 (more contenders for the Top Ten), I have consistently loved books that I've read when I've been sick in bed. In these fractured, frantic times, it's rare to have several unbroken hours and days in which to do nothing but read. In my sickbed I read as I expect writers intended me to: in a concentrated, unbroken period of time in which the interior world of the book swells and takes over the real world. The characters are rounded, the landscapes three-dimensional, the plot twists comprehensible and satisfying.

So often, though, I'm not sick in bed and don't have the time to read more than a few pages at night before sleep pulls me under. It is a rare book that wins the battle against drooping eyelids. I've fallen asleep over Austen and Atwood, Wilkie Collins and Philip Pullman. Many times I've known that I would have enjoyed a book more if I'd given it the chance of a fair chunk of uninterrupted time. In short, liking or not liking a book depends a great deal on the quality of time we make for it. That is as important, if not more so, than the writing itself, and can make all the difference between three stars and five stars, a Top Ten or nowhere near the charts.

Asking someone what his or her Top Ten books are is a very twenty-first-century question. It's hard to imagine getting Austen, George Eliot, Tolstoy, Woolf, or Faulkner to name their Top Ten reads. Even recent venerables like Margaret Atwood and Toni Morrison would very likely give the question short shrift. (Morrison once replied thus to a nervous journalist's question about whether she uses a pen and paper or computer when she writes: "You really have collapsed, haven't you?" Imagine her response to a Top Ten request!) Writers from the past were unlikely to be sympathetic to the current thinking that shapes such a question: the desire not to take the time to delve but to know someone at a glance. Jane Austen easily used half a page describing someone's eyes; she would not appreciate summarizing her reading tastes in ten titles.

But in this time-tight world, where *New Yorker* articles are getting shorter and newspaper interviews often turn into questionnaires about favorite foods, our greatest fear (in five words or less), and how we would like to be remembered, the Top Ten makes the perfect sound bite. It saves readers time: We assume we know someone and so don't have to read the whole interview, much less, God forbid, their books.

I suspect past writers would also sense the contradiction grating behind the question. We want to know someone's Top Ten as an encapsulation of a writer, and yet we also expect the list to reflect a kind of Platonic ideal of writing. Perhaps someone else could get away with listing a Danielle Steele in his or her Top Ten, but a writer would be laughed out of town. We are expected to list our favorite books, yes, but those are really meant to be the best books as well. People may accept that our lists change, for all of the reasons I've discussed, but they do expect each list to be sound. That makes it impossible to answer honestly, which is why Austen would dismiss the question with a witty, self-deprecating remark, and Atwood would probably answer briefly and caustically enough to make any questioner feel foolish.

In the end, the Top Ten list does not give us a full picture of a person, but rather ten slices of his or her life, as viewed optimistically by him or her at the moment of compilation—say, October 1, 2004, at 11:30 A.M. Certainly books are better, more sophisticated indicators of character than, say, shoes or restaurants or vacation destinations. But even the "best" book— whatever that really means—is not as complicated as we are. A list is not enough. If I gave my optician an honest answer about my eyesight I would take as long as Jane Austen to describe my eyes. My appointment with her would take longer, and cost more, but I might well see more clearly as a result.

PART FOUR

• • •

THE FUTURE

A COMPUTER
ATE MY BOOK

Douglas Rushkoff

Books have souls. Or so romantics like me tend to think. Neither the Internet nor computers really threaten the book as an art form. But if we're to believe the latest rumblings from publishing industry journals, author's panels, and librarians' conferences around the world, the book business is in terrible danger. And so are magazines, newspapers, and anything else printed on a page.

According to the defenders of literate culture and their high-priced sociologists, Americans are reading less and, as a result, thinking less. The preponderance of electronic media, from the Internet to interactive gaming, has apparently seduced would-be readers away from their books, to all of our peril.

So why am I smiling?

Frankly, I don't see the problem, here. So far, the Internet has been nothing but great for my own writing career, and those of just about every other writer I know. Even better, the Internet serves to disseminate our ideas—which is the real reason anyone worth his or her pulp should be writing in the first place. By putting chapters of our work and even whole books on our Web sites, we allow people to get access to our writing who might not be able to afford it otherwise. As a result, our ideas more easily become part of everyday conversation. Our words have more impact, because we let them spread over the Internet, for free.

About 25,000 different people regularly read my daily posts on my blog. No, I don't have ads or get any revenue for writing it—but I do get to converse with my readers in the comments section, find out when I'm saying something that provokes them, and use my writing to establish relationships with people who may not be able to afford the time or money to read my books. Blogs are also a great way for writers to check in with our readers and for them to check in with us more frequently and immediately than the every year or two it takes to write and publish a book.

Of course, all this additional conversation and reader service only makes our books more likely candidates for school curricula and libraries, not to mention individual purchases. This means we can pay our rent more easily. And so can our editors and publishers. So works the "gift economy."

Instead of celebrating this fact, the publishing industry's decisionmakers are quivering. My current U.S. publishers *still* won't let me release the electronic versions of my works for free. They are afraid of losing sales. And I'd venture their fear is costing them a lot of money, in the long run. The only exceptions, so far, are books about "open source" and "creative commons," which can't very well be held back without undermining their very premise.

Most book publishers still look at the Napster phenomenon as an advance warning of what will soon happen to their industry: People will pass around digital copies of books and never pay for them anymore! As a result, according to this logic, there will be no money left to pay for writers—not to mention editors and everyone else who works in publishing-as-we-know-it.

These dire predictions are not unlike those made by silly record executives in the 1930s who, so fearful of the effects of radio broadcasting on their sales, actually forbade their recordings to be played over the radio! That's right—record labels carried a warning that broadcasting them was illegal! Within a couple of decades, of course, record companies were paying DJs to get their records played on the air.

That's because media don't actually steal from each other. They feed each other. Just as hearing a song on the radio might provoke a person to buy a CD, reading text by authors online can motivate people to buy their actual books.

In the best cases, it can lead to a kind of renaissance. Just when it appears that a new medium is going to replace its predecessor, we tend to figure out the true value of the older. Experts thought that the videocassette would put the traditional movie house out of business. Instead, it turned the general public into amateur film historians, while giving cinemas an idea of what they can offer us that videos can't: giant screens, THX sound, glamorous lobbies, and an evening out of the house. It made us like movies *more*.

So far, computers haven't made people read less; they make us read more. Most of the kids I've met online have astonishing literacy skills. No matter how visual the World Wide Web might get in its interface, it's still a word-based medium when you follow anything through or try to glean any real information.

And because Internet users need to type pretty much everything they wish to communicate, they have developed some pretty clever twists on language. Online interaction actually makes a person's writing better. I can tell when I've received e-mail from people raised on the Internet because their sentences are dense with innuendo, compensating for the limited time and keystrokes they can devote to the task. Kids online today write much better than I did at their age. Or at least with greater density of thought.

A new medium only replaces an old one if it does *everything* better. The telephone does pretty much everything better than the telegraph. Computers can do a few things better than books can. They're better at rapid searching and retrieval of information, so they are better as encyclopedias, dictionaries, or articles databases. But that's not everything.

Real books are more than mere repositories for information. They are objects, and they are meant to be experienced as such. The function of a dictionary is to provide the meaning of a word. The function of a book is to provide a reading experience. It's more than a transmission of data: It's a transmission of essence.

Not that computers don't transmit their own sort of essence, too. Narrative computer games from *Everquest* to *The Sims* proved so successful because they captured something essential about the seemingly random, user-directed navigational path of a computer world. *Everquest* was a user-improvised fantasy role-playing experience while the Sims were practically an emergent life form. Freed from the linear constraints of traditional literary fiction, digital storytellers could allow their readers/users to make discoveries for themselves.

I've even experimented, myself, canceling a contract for a novel in order to be able to post the entire thing online. I invited readers to comment on the text as if it were an object found by anthropologists two hundred years in the future. Eleven hundred users created their own footnotes to the text, in the voices of fictional anthropologists explaining words like *Microsoft* and *profit* to their contemporaries, who had presumably evolved beyond such notions. Eleven hundred strangers, all contributing to the development of a piece of literature, thanks to the Internet.

But just because the word is alive and well doesn't necessarily mean that the printed page, bound to hundreds of others and glued into a cardboard cover, will survive, too. There are only so many eyeball hours in a day, the pessimists warn, and book reading takes up too many for it to remain a viable format. Digital text retrieval already allows an entire text to be downloaded in seconds, and then read on a palmtop or cell phone. That format is more conducive to the kinds of briefs and summaries that publishers like Harvard Business Press are already favoring over the old-fashioned book-length work.

Luckily, people buy books as much to own them as to read or play them. Books have "object value," look good on coffee tables, and are a lot easier to lend to Grandma. Plus, they're a hell of a lot easier to read in bed, or on an airplane, or on the subway.

Books offer a different experience than digital media. This experience has as much to do with the pages and ink as it does with the words themselves. A book has totemic value. Like a photograph or a piece of jewelry, the impression of ink on paper creates physical connection with its author.

This is why the publishing industry, in response to the advent of digital text, has begun to emphasize the design and production of the books themselves. Most publishers now use acid-free "archival" quality paper and devote more time and energy to the choice of typeface and cover art. Smaller publishers create limited editions and "high touch" designs that appeal to many senses. Likewise, we authors are being forced to realize that our books better communicate something more than a Web page does. We have to understand what a book can do and either fulfill that purpose or quit cutting down trees.

Computers have reminded us of the special ability of books to provide a kind of experience you can't get anywhere else. And although leading book publishers like to blame the Internet for their own waning profits, it is an entirely different set of high-tech pressures posing problems for printed prose.

For instance, the Internet is already changing the way these physical objects are distributed. The book industry's dominance over the production and dissemination of our works could soon very well be coming to an end. It's an inefficient, laborious, and time-consuming process that eats up 85 percent of a book's cover price. They've never had to worry about justifying their own existence, because we authors have never had an alternative form of distribution, until now. Enter Amazon.com, Xlibris, and iUniverse.

These services combine to allow anyone to write a book, print to order, and sell it right over the Web. The only hurdle left is publicity. (Ask any author you know how much the publisher actually contributed to the publicity effort for his or her last book. These days, many of us pay for our own tours and ads.) From the up-and-comer's perspective, the Internet does not threaten print media. It only threatens to disintermediate the dead wood.

But let's be honest—publishers won't be going down without a fight. A few of them may still have enough skill in both literature and business to rise to the occasion that the Internet offers. They may be forced to serve authors instead of enslaving them, but that's a lesson many of them need to learn anyway—just like the recording industry's worst offenders.

Instead of serving their authors' need for editorial expertise, the publishers have relegated some of their most vital choices to computers, exacerbating the book's inevitable slide toward consumer commodity. When sales data and spreadsheet software determine everything from acquisition to distribution, it's no wonder the short-term stock value of the parent media conglomerate takes precedence over the long-term health of literature. Computers, which could have made the industry more responsive, are instead being programmed to discourage new growth. "Mid-list" titles are shunned in favor of blockbusters, which are actually less dependably profitable, considering the investment required, and make for a less stable revenue stream.

So publishers lose money on higher volume and then blame the Internet for a loss of interest in books. It is not the readers who have forgotten about the soul of the book; it is the publishers. Computers don't kill books; people do.

Ironically, my own books about new media and cyberculture have themselves been outsmarted by computers. My first book—one of the first books about technoculture—had a cover made of such a hi-tech shiny material that no cash register's scanner could read the bar code. Sales clerks had to enter the price of the book manually, often without entering the book's computer-coded ISBN number. Most stores had no record of the sales of my book and thus no automatic reordering of more copies. Until the problem was fixed, every store was out of stock, yet the book had close to zero registered sales. This, in turn, translated into a lower recorded total sale of books and smaller orders the next time around.

Another breathlessly protechnology book of mine, *Children of Chaos*, had its title changed at the last minute by my U.S. publisher's sales department, whose computer-aided market research had determined that books with the word *chaos* in the title weren't selling as well as they once had. They renamed the book *Playing the Future* but forgot to tell anyone. The publisher thought if it simply entered the change of title into one of its own computers, all the bookstores and libraries would somehow implement the change, too. Oops.

None of the bookstores, not even the big chains, found out about this new title. Their computers simply waited for the original book to show up in stock. When my retitled book arrived at bookstores and warehouses throughout the United States, most of them were promptly returned to the publisher unopened. They hadn't ordered a book with that title! Everyone who went to a store asking for my book by its original title was told it hadn't come in yet. Everyone who went asking for it by the new title was told that it didn't exist. It wasn't in the computer, so it didn't exist in today's book world.

Two months went by before someone figured out how to reenter the title of the book in the distribution computer networks, but by then it was too late. Ordering programs dictate that if a book hasn't sold well in the first three months, it shouldn't be reordered. (Luckily, though it was unavailable in stores, thanks to Internet and computerized sales the book ended up becoming one of the top ten "special ordered" books of the year.) As in any industry, computers only help when they are used by people. The information and analysis they provide us with are extremely valuable but must be contextualized by real people who understand the markets and media in which they are being employed.

So far, this doesn't seem to be the case. Advances on new books are proffered based solely on sales of one's last book. So my writing a niche book on ways of reinterpreting Torah in an open source context (not a likely mass market paperback) ends up determining the size of advance I get for my soon-to-be best seller business book. Then again, the sales of my best-selling business book become the basis for the advance on my next cyberdelic novel, so it all comes out in the wash. Still, I'd love to hear that publishers were using a bit of their own decisionmaking powers rather than just depending on the data streams coming from the mainframes at Barnes and Noble headquarters.

Though I've been burned by them, I still hold no grudge against the computers that ate my book or any other—just against the people who let them do it.

THE SLIPPERY SLOPE
TO MARGARITAVILLE

Vivien Mejia

Tan trash. That's what I like to call myself when I order in beer and pizza to the horror of my gastronomically snobby friends. I'm first-generation American by way of Colombia, S.A., thus the "tan" part. I'm one of those hopelessly mixed-up kids who still believe in the ever-more-tarnished American Dream through franchising (I'd like to open a Petco/Taco Bell combo) but can trace back my roots twenty generations straight to the Spanish Inquisition and Fitzcarraldo in the jungle by the wide green Amazon. Oh, yeah, and I'm a writer by trade. Lately, a "Latina" writer. Somehow the moniker that once garnered me nothing but disdain from the brats at Coral Gables Elementary School now gets me gigs. "Sure, sure, I'm Latina," I say. As if somehow, by default, the lilt in my last name has imbued me with a level of expertise about one-fifth of the world's population someone who isn't Latino can't possibly fathom. And so goes the writing—from what Latinos eat for breakfast to how Latinos vote, I've covered the gamut in my essays and have called myself an expert with nary a doubt in my voice, if not my head. I have to constantly remind myself and others I can only squeak out my own tiny voice from my corner of this vast literary landscape, and it has nothing to do with beans and rice, Spanglish, or even, sadly, salsa dancing.

On the contrary, it's a wasteland of strip malls, MTV commercials, and J-Lo, just like every other schmo, white, black or brown. I even pepper my language with Yiddish for crying out loud—too many years in Hollywood, I guess. And therein lies the rub: The "Latino" market *is* the American market; they're one and the same. And while the Latino demographic continues to grow by leaps and bounds in the United States, it's a bit of an artificial barometer. Part of the problem is the slippery slope one gets onto when describing the "typical Latino." With a couple of dozen Spanish-speaking countries around the world, each with a host of disparate influences on their fundamentally Spanish foundation, from African, to indigenous, to European, to Asian, it's no wonder it's hard to herd the vanguard that ends up in the United States into one convenient marketing slice o' pie.

I remember back in the day, short on cash, I'd joined one of those focus group agencies, where on occasion, for fifty or seventy bucks, I'd be called in to blab about my toilet paper habits or what kind of car I'd like to drive. More and more they'd begun to favor me because I could speak Spanish and filled an ever-growing demand for "Latino" consumers. I'd listed I owned pets but had left it at that. One day, I was called by an officious young man who asked me if I owned a dog. I didn't, but replied vaguely, hoping to still get the gig. "I *could* own a dog, " I said. "OK, well, this is the most important part," he said. "Would you say you speak Spanish at home as your primary language?" "Hmm, well, I live alone, so usually I'm not really speaking (out loud anyway)." Good enough. Before I knew it I was with ten other women arguing about what kind of dog food to feed little Paco, my imaginary pug. Some of these women had arrived by bus and were feeding their dogs scraps from the table; a couple had business suits on and were feeding their pups something off the supermarket shelf. By the end of the session, I'd become what is known as an "influencer" and was instructing the women to shop at specialty pet stores that can really address a dog's changing needs as he grows older. I'm not sure what was deduced by the group moderator besides that it was going to be a long night.

At the risk of sounding too business-like, I will say that the Latino population is at its core a vertically integrated socioeconomically divergent population. We are simply not homogeneous and therefore create the same kind of challenges publishers, advertisers, and so on have faced when trying to market to the Asian population, for example, who, though ethnographically homogeneous, come from different cultural and linguistic centers. I mean, come on; half "my peeps" don't even *like* each other. Just ask a Venezuelan about a Colombian or an Argentinean about anyone outside Europe or Buenos Aires, for that matter, and you'll get some pretty un-PC commentary. And so to assume a uniformity of thought on anything from music to religion to literature is a flawed proposition at best.

"Well, then, how come Spanish-language television and Spanish-language entertainment are a multi-billion dollar enterprise?" you might ask. I'll tell you why: Español, baby, Español.

The beautiful comfort of a shared language can unite much more than it should: Suddenly opinions on so many of life's infinite choices seem to be soothed by the sound of the mother tongue. That tongue is being spoken more and more in the United States by recent immigrants, and it is perhaps that aspect of the Latino market that should be embraced and serviced more by traditional translation and Spanish content material than by trying to appeal to the netherworld of English-speaking first- and second-generation Latinos like myself. Because the truth of the matter is we're reading the *New Yorker* (or the *National Enquirer*, or both) along with everybody else. And here's the crux: We're reading them in English.

And we're writing in English.

Confusing, I know. Why do you think over 65 percent of first- and second-generation Latinos have been in some form of psychotherapy? Actually, I made that figure up, but it can't be too far from the truth. I mean, the experience, as I'm sure has been related ad infinitum, of the immigrant-raised child, dreaming in one language but speaking in another, is, well, crazy-making. And the literature written by the Junot Diazes and Julia Alvarezes of the world *is* filled with that mysterious and singular combination of Latin poetry and American angst found nowhere else. But let us remember that, though uniquely fascinating and deserving of merit, this is a wholly different and separate enterprise than needing to translate Tide commercials into Spanish for *Vanidades* magazine. And I might add, if there was some way to check, I would venture to say the audience for Diaz or Sandra Cisneros might not necessarily be too different from the audience for, say, Alice Sebold or Wally Lamb.

There is a kind of "cultural tourism" that takes place among literature-loving types. I remember a friend telling me she connected with Latinos more after reading *The House on Mango Street*. She liked the way slang and Spanish were sprinkled into the narrative. She said she felt as if she now understood how "Latinos" spoke at home. I said nothing. What was the point of explaining to her I grew up in a household where Spanglish was slapped down like the lowest form of virus. Where I was taught a "pure Castilian" and wasn't allowed to mix with what was perceived as the teeming masses by my elitist family. Where English was not spoken *at all*, but my brother and I devoured English storybooks at night like contraband *Playboys*. But that is my singular story and I don't necessarily expect anyone else to share it. Even if I did write about it. So, no, I didn't bother to explain to my highly educated, liberal, well-read friend that her statement would be the equivalent of me saying I understood how southerners lived now because I read *Bastard Out of Carolina* or how the French made love after reading *The Story of O*—OK, maybe not *The Story of O*, maybe *Spy in the House of Love*.

In any case, yes, Cisneros wrote a book filled with a narrative reality worthy of praise, but I can safely assume she meant it to be used as an allegory and not a travelogue or documentary on the lives of every person of Latin descent in the United States. Nevertheless, my friend's overly eager embrace of *Mango Street* might help explain the uptick in sales of certain Latino authors, as the American book-reading public grapples with trying to understand this vast group of people taking up residence in their neighborhoods, churches, and schools. But it might also explain why Latinos aren't necessarily the demographic buying the books themselves. The Latino Americans' experience is as varied and singular as any non-Latinos' experience, and chances are they, too, would be "cultural tourists" in Oscar Hijuelos's Cuban-American reality, just as he might be a tourist in Alisa Valdes-Rodriguez's *Dirty Girls Social Club*. Meaning, while I could be moved by Cisneros, I don't necessarily know if I relate to her protagonist any more than I do to Bridget Jones: Unfortunately for me, I fit into *that* demographic as well.

None of this is to say there isn't something particularly telling and vivid in the ever-growing list of Latino-American writers (vs. Latin American) who are currently writing about their ever-varied experiences growing up hyphenates in this country. Though their stories are as differentiated as Danielle Steele is from Dave Eggers, they are, in a fashion, documenting the bizarre and eternal alchemy of north meets south, or yin meets yang, salsa meets meatloaf, and so on. As they do so, much of the writing feels a bit—Dare I say?—mutant.

This mix of English and Spanish, and hip-hop, and Chinese, and French and, and, and . . . is staggering. It only proves further the prescience of cult film *Blade Runner*'s vision of a world where, for instance, Los Angelenos would be speaking a dialect consisting of several languages and everyone would look mildly Asian-Latino-Anglo-African-American. It's dizzying and it's exciting. We are indeed moving in a new direction.

This new breed of writer who dreams in Spanish but writes in English, who eats Captain Crunch but dances merengue, who knows Marc Antony but doesn't know Simon Bolívar, is a reality. A reality only mirrored by the general population. There will always be messengers, but eventually the masses do follow. Joe West Virginia may not know who Isabel Allende is, but I guarantee you he knows how to make a mean margarita and can probably appreciate pot stickers, too. And isn't that strange and funny and weird and . . . American?

I'm reminded of Baz Luhrmann's *Romeo + Juliet*, with its postmodern Mexico City sets. Who would've thought that quickly mutating and churning world of multiethnicity, borderline baroque pollution, and overpopulation could be so romantic? And yet it was. It was downright darling. I always wanted to write a touching, terribly tragic love story set in a Jack in the Box. Like Hemingway's short story "Hills like White Elephants," our doomed couple would talk about life, death, and romance, only they would be doing it over french fries, egg rolls, and diet cola as they watched traffic gridlock on Wilshire Boulevard. Strangely enough, though the strangeness of our future may seem so clear to us right now, I have no doubt there will come a time when this topic will seem as provincial and quaint as when Cervantes and Dante were scandalizing the world with their vernacular takes on the Latin in *Don Quixote* and *Inferno*. In their heyday, writing in Spanish and Italian, respectively, both languages considered bastardizations of Latin, they took their world by storm. I'm certain they were being called the equivalent of "tan trash" back in their day. And so I can only hope to walk in their footsteps proudly, a Marlboro on my lips, a *cerveza* in my hand.

ANDREW KRUCOFF AND
THE AMAZING PAPER WEBLOG

Elizabeth Spiers

Blogging is dead, and a baby-faced data analyst named Andrew Krucoff killed it. That's the conclusion I reach after spending a grim, rainy Sunday afternoon on the Lower East Side listening to Krucoff explain why he's turning his Weblog, TheOtherPage.com, into a print publication that he and his friend Chris Gage would produce from the bedroom of his Lower East Side apartment. Krucoff is thirty-three with messy brown hair and mischievous blue eyes. His red-and-white-striped shirt clashes with his argyle socks and Camper bowling shoes in an Elvis Costello-ish nerdy-yet-hip fashion that is more-or-less indigenous to the neighborhood, and as he explains the process, Gage, a lanky thirty-two-year-old blond with glasses and studs in his ears, sits on a stool next to the door, inserting the occasional footnote.

You've probably never heard of Krucoff or Gage, but among New York bloggers, they are semifamous. They may not be the A list, but they're definitely in the upper echelons of the B list, and in this tiny, incestuous corner of cyberspace, B list counts for something. Bloggers like Krucoff (but not specifically Krucoff) have been media darlings for a couple of years now, and if you were reading newspapers, watching TV, or leaving your house to interact with the outside world, you may have noticed that there were bloggers at the 2004 Democratic National Convention. Subsequently, you may also have noticed that there were also bloggers at the 2004 Republican National Convention, bloggers blogging the presidential debates, bloggers blogging Dan Rather and forged memos, bloggers blogging the 2004 presidential election returns, and bloggers blogging other bloggers. In fact, I don't really see how you could have avoided it. When I type *blog* into Nexis's news database and specify articles written in the "previous 30 days," I get an error message that says, "Your search is interrupted because it will return over 1,000 documents."

Theoretically, I should be the last person on earth to find saturation coverage of blogs annoying. Blogging has been good to me, and were it not for blogging, I would probably be putting together valuation models for tech companies instead of writing professionally (the latter of which is much more enjoyable, if you're wondering). But lately I've begun to think of my relationship with blogging as a misguided love affair that ended amicably—the sort of thing where you wake up one day and realize that you don't really know the person sleeping next to you, that you somehow failed to notice that he chews with his mouth open, and that you deeply suspect that were it not for the share in the Hamptons, the mutual friends, and the first few months of enjoyable sex, you might not even be friends. Who are you? And why did I ever love you in the first place?

When I arrive at Krucoff's two bedroom on Stanton Street, half the lights are out because one of the electrical outlets has been inexplicably shooting sparks across the kitchen and Krucoff and Gage, tired of tiptoeing around it, lest they be electrocuted, have cut power to that part of the room. I'm curious about what this seemingly oxymoronic "print blog" is, and would like to find out before they inadvertently burn the place down. Irony, or attempted irony, infuses most of Krucoff's extracurricular activities, and his latest project has all the signs of yet another effort to be the Johnny Knoxville of the Internet. He and Gage use the word *retarded* as a derogatory rather than medical adjective, and *dude*, though sparingly used, is frequently implied. They explain that they plan to recruit people to write blog entries, which they will then edit using Quark publishing software, print ("We'll put it on *résumé* paper!"), photocopy, then mail to subscribers via the U.S. Postal Service. The print blog is, unbelievably, exactly what it sounds like. "The best thing," says Gage, "is that I keep telling everybody I'm trying to get involved that we want to do stories about dune buggies and the low-flying helicopters that chase them! That's so retarded, it's awesome!"

I met Krucoff a little over a year ago, when he began writing amusing fake interviews with fictional "young Manhattanites" for Lasagnafarm.com (another blog he maintains) in an attempt to get linked by Gawker.com, a Manhattan media gossip Weblog that I was editing at the time.

"It's all about getting a reaction from someone else," they insist and point to their mock obsession with fellow blogger Lockhart Steele as evidence that provoking other people for their own amusement is part of their schtick. Steele is the managing editor of Cottage & Gardens Publications, which produces *Hamptons Cottages and Gardens*, *Palm Beach Cottages and Gardens*, and the soon-to-be launched *Connecticut Cottages and Gardens*. In keeping with his professional interests, he runs a blog about Manhattan real estate called Curbed.com and his personal Weblog, LockhartSteele.com, is best known for its extensive knowledge of the neighborhood in which he and Krucoff both live. A sampling of LockhartSteele.com posts might include some news about a restaurant opening, FreshDirect's local delivery route, or the gentrification of the area.

"I'll be honest," Krucoff sniffs. "I'm friends with him, but at the beginning, it was just the idea of this guy named Lockhart Steele, and like, he's the voice of the Lower East Side? It was offensive! It was offensive to my forefathers, and they're immigrants! I just figured I'd go ahead and take him down."

"I started writing about the Lower East Side, and people seemed to be interested in that," says Steele, a preppy St. Paul's/Brown grad who acknowledges that he and Krucoff are friends and that the rivalry is entirely tongue-in-cheek. "Maybe because there's a dearth of good local media, or maybe because people are bored out of their fucking minds." He laughs when I ask him what he thinks about Krucoff's print blog. "It's all a lot of hot air as far as I'm concerned until I see something in my hands."

When Krucoff began lobbing virtual grenades in Steele's direction, Steele's blog was getting considerably more hits than Krucoff's. "I am amazed Lockhart Steele is given a credible voice on [Lower East Side] issues," he blogged. "I fear most people do not know the devil lurking behind those semi-retarded updates of block-by-block FreshDirect availability." Lurking devil Steele responded to Krucoff's assault, calling him a "nonblogger" (presumably an insult) posting "lonely" commentary on his "sad little site"—and invariably sending Krucoff more readers than he had before. Krucoff didn't use the same tactic with me, but when I linked to him from Gawker, he got more traffic and then began creating more content that was appropriate for Gawker in order to get linked again and get even more traffic.

This, in a nutshell, is how blogs work. Bloggers typically write some sort of commentary linking to something else— usually a news story or another blog post. Someone else links to that post, and someone else to that one. Eventually there's a discernible thread of discussion spread over multiple Web logs.

"Blogs are conversations," says Jeff Jarvis, the president of Condé Nast's Advance.net operations, founder of *Entertainment Weekly*, and blog proprietor of Buzzmachine.com, who says he finds himself attending journalism confabs "not as media man, but as blog boy. What does that mean? It means that once a story is published, it's no longer just fish wrap; it's no longer over. That's only the beginning." Jarvis believes that in a post–Jayson Blair environment, blogging sublimates big media by subjecting them to an extra layer of scrutiny and creating a dialogue around the subject matter.

But the implications of this for bloggers like Andrew Kru-coff and blogs like Gawker is that the "conversation" turns into a series of in-jokes, whispered among a small group of people, and the end result is either funny or exceedingly irritating. "Writers writing about other writers writing about other writing," says Neal Pollack, an Austin-based humorist who stopped blogging after the self-referentiality got to be too much. "It's just pathetic," he says. "I hope it goes away. It's not going to, but I hope it does."

Peter Merholz, a San Francisco–based Web designer often credited with inventing the world *blog* by changing *Weblog* to *We blog*, famously stopped blogging last March. He has since started again, but at the time, he wrote, "I realized that, I really hadn't anything to say. I was posting out of obligation to an audience, not because the spirit moved me." He added:

> I was also growing increasingly frustrated with the echo chamber effect of weblogs. A meme drifts out there, and then 38 different people post their take on that meme, and they all link to each other, and, as a reader, you bounce from post to post, the semantic feedback growing until it's deafening. I needed to remove myself from that for a while. To prune a tree. To look on as my g/f and another friend weeded my garden. To get licked in the face by a dog.

The echo chamber effect and the in-jokes make it easy for bloggers to get sucked into online pseudocommunities that appear to outsiders as virtual cliques. "To get to the good stuff," wrote the *Washington Post*'s Jennifer Howard in a recent article on blogs, "you have to wade through more and more self-congratulation and mutual admiration."

"I feel like, it kind of eats itself, cycles in on itself after a while," says Pollack. "It's just so damn meaningless that it makes my teeth hurt."

"Part of my sabbatical has been [the result of] burnout on weblogging and that whole circle that I've been in," says Meg Hourihan, the cofounder of Blogger.com, a popular blogging software application that was sold to Google in 2002. "I just felt so close to it all. And everybody seems like they're talking about the same thing." Meg is still blogging but has doubts about whether the conversations in which she finds herself participating are accomplishing anything productive. "I just kept feeling like, 'I don't even think this stuff is important in the real world,'" adds Hourihan. "Or I can't even tell if it's important. I have a sense that maybe it's not and I can't get any perspective because I'm in so close. It's like I already know all these people and they're saying all the same stuff. And I start thinking, 'I don't even know if I care about weblogs anymore.'" But Meg is still blogging, because she has the freedom to take a break from it when necessary: "I always just sort of do it when I want and don't do it when I don't feel like it."

I can sympathize with Neal and Meg. A few months ago, I got burned out on blogging because I got sick of the tiny blogo-sphere conflicts that seemed to balloon into real-world melodramas, the circular arguments and the pettiness that sometimes occur online because people don't have to talk to each other face-to-face. So I stopped doing it. My blood pressure returned to a normal level and I didn't miss it. I got my reading and writing elsewhere.

I started blogging in the first place because I liked to write and have always been a voracious reader. Blogging provides an unlimited supply of both.

The reading habit started early. When I was nine or ten, my mother would drive me to the Wetumpka, Alabama, public library on a near-weekly basis, and I'd check out an armful of books and then proceed to devour them at a rate of one or two a day. Then I'd beg her to take me back for more. My parents weren't big readers (unless you count the Bible—they're evangelical Christians) and the excess seemed a bit dysfunctional, so when it was determined that I'd been spending too much time in my room with "my nose in a book," I'd be instructed to go play outside, like a normal kid. But to my mother's credit, she kept driving me to the library.

That reading habit never really died, and as I made my way through college at Duke University after high school, my addiction to the information and narrative formerly provided by books was severely exacerbated by the Internet. The public library just didn't provide the same kind of instant gratification.

I also found myself writing more, which seems to happen any time my reading volume increases. I've always written for my own enjoyment—bad fiction, bad poetry, bad journal entries, and so on—and when I found myself stuck in an antiseptic office in New York, staring morosely at Excel spreadsheets six years later, I wrote to keep myself sane. I was working in finance and discovered blogging software while doing research on content management technologies and set up my own blog to test it out. Soon I was writing bad fiction, bad poetry, and bad journal entries again—and posting them on the Internet.

Shortly after, other bloggers began responding, linking to my posts and sending me e-mail. I got hooked on the constant feedback and the way bloggers would continually reference earlier points, creating narrative and structure for what would otherwise be discreet little units of disconnected information. *This* was why I fell in love with blogging.

The text was alive, and that was exciting, not just to me, but to all the people who were affected, including the media outlets that covered it. It was a shiny, new thing, and different from anything else that existed in media because it was truly interactive. And without that, it was nothing.

Without the interactivity, there was no way to respond to what you were reading and no way for your readers to respond to what you were writing. Without the cross-references and the dialogue, the text would have stood alone and there would have been a finality to it. It would have been like a book.

But at some point, the cross-references seem more like incest. Krucoff, the world's first print blogger, finds the incestuousness amusing, and the idea for the print blog originally followed the rejection of another idea that would have both satirized and legitimized the idea of a blogger clique. "I was toying around with the idea of password-protecting [the blog] and making it the Soho House of blogs," he says, referring to a trendy private club in New York's meatpacking district. "And then we were only going to invite certain people," adds Gage. "And you could only get in with a recommendation. It just cracked us up. The whole online blogging world is so insular and everybody knows each other and everything; it just seemed to take it to the natural retarded next step."

Krucoff and Gage are enumerating the logistics of sending out their first print blog and attempting to plot a business model to match their new, more expensive medium. They plan to underwrite the cost of materials and thirty-seven-cent stamps by selling advertising, and Gage, who is getting married, insists from recent experience that licking two hundred envelopes isn't nearly as unpleasant as it seems.

"Worst comes down to it," says Krucoff, "Mrs. Gage will sponsor this with yearbook type ads. You know, 'This picture is brought to you by Mrs. Gage!'"

"We'll get Lockhart's mom first!" interjects Gage.

"Yeah! We'll get Lock's mom!" says Krucoff.

I wait for the inevitable high five, but it doesn't come.

The idea that traditional print media can beget blogging isn't new, but a print publication derived from a blog is the ultimate rejection of blogging as a strange curiosity that exists in a media vacuum. That Andrew Krucoff would want to turn his blog into a print publication indicates that blogging has officially come full circle and that those lines have been blurred. It's also a retreat from the incestuous aspects of blogging that were initially attractive and later repulsive to me.

That's not to say that blogging won't enjoy some level of uniqueness, or that the echo chamber will go away. But the media coverage of blogging, the novelty, and the "other"-ness of it will. The blog as a shiny new thing, separate and apart from the rest of media, is dead.

There are still a few things wrong with a "print blog." It's ostensibly a twisted misunderstanding of the technology—like the Marshall McLuhan anecdote about the early years of printing presses, when people would take mass-produced books to scribes to be copied and illustrated, unable to adapt to new publishing conventions.

But maybe on some level, Krucoff is a genius. And to be fair, it's not his first print project. A few months ago, he and Gage produced a publication called *Book of Wages*, which they printed from an electronic file and distributed at a party they held at their apartment. Krucoff claims that this is where they "really hit their retarded stride." The book was a parody of the recently published *Book of Ages*—a gift-book compendium of age-related statistics, authored by one Mr. Lockhart Steele.

EPILOGUE:
MY WORDS CONSUME ME

Nico Cary, age nineteen

Sometimes my words consume me
I fold only writing the cold deep breath holding days
Lay knees to chest
waiting to be born
like dawn breaks freely expressing to an open sky
summer dries into fall
White walls ask for brown skin subservient minds
and sometimes my words consume me
unworldly
the binary dualism that separates worlds she
moves random
like other like difference
natural she moves
only discernible with discourse, with this coarse
*   and projected fixed fear*
ignoble and noble

savage be language, mercantilism, even
development so called
a sexually fantasy beat against white walls
she moves
gently to the melodic murmur of neo-colonialism
So real it's surreal
So real it's surreal bicentric ill will and the distance
 of eye-sized fears
I fear I feel never scraping the back of my throat
cynical
I fold only writing the cold deep
Breath holding days unlearned space
it's bent molded broken at thought
things
fall apart
the opposition of all being like wet feet independent
 of subservient mind move
tomorrow builds up until I can't swallow like desperate
 on a bottle top curve
and my side hurts
like unengaged words to a barren page
the rust colored burn aged in eye-sized fears like
6 billion prayers to an open sky and the dead sea that
 holds it to faith
Like satin between a rock and a hard place
Faith stretches on long face and bends as dawn breaks
with the morose of nameless me precociously uninhibited
Enclosed between white walls asking for brown skin and
 subservient minds
Like the universe she can back spin
But I know cosmology can't explain this

fermentative anguish
permanent vacant eyes
Or swollen hands clinging to the opposition of all
    things being
Me in my skin like mid-summer rain sounds
self-doubt is melodic in faith
recapitulated through escape routes as fetuses
    underdeveloped fist raised in damaged womb
Six feet of earth and the deepest maroon
Her worst in vain when the thirst is plain my side hurts
    the same against the grain I move like we feet groove
    to freedom's ring
Sometimes my words consume me
Like unduly elected officials and political platitudes
Cold deep breath pursuing cynicism unto the depth
    of mid-Atlantic ridge
It's memory unto the depth of psychological rape
Or faith as unlearned space
Diversity like summer drying into fall
Like agoraphobic birds to an open sky and white
    wall comfort
The unencumbered smile of random she moving gently
    to the melodic murmur of neo-colonialism
body sway melancholic though
I can't call it yo
the distance eye-sized fears or clairvoyant stares into
    the dark
unlearned space marks the unknown self
Broken at thought
when reconfigured words emerge at the chance of
    self-destruction drop

Like
fuck that nigga
my side hurts
fuck that nigga
and my side hurts
Like the rust colored burn aged in eye-sized fears
so real I'm scared only linguistics prepared it's nothing
When the surrealistic moment or
bare bone torment tears at the divide it's murderous
pitted against white walls its ruthless
abstruse movement sway body melancholic
I can't call the distance words consume me
and I can't call it
The distance faith and that nigga possess
a name and Guess
Unlearned space and cynicism
Clairvoyance and fear
My words and I
a closed fist to an open sky
vacant eyes and neo-colonialism
The precision is ever new
subtle change
mid-summer rain her worst in vain
she escapes to aged brick city thick
This is when my words consume me
and my side hurts but we keep moving and my side hurts
   but we keep moving
and I can't call it

ACKNOWLEDGMENTS

Big thank yous go around the world to all the authors who gave so generously of their time and talents; my agent, Jud Laghi (who "knows how we roll"); editor and fellow midwesterner Megan Hustad for her faith, tenacity, and level head; Iris Richmond, Holly Bemiss, and everyone at Basic Books, who were a dream to work for and with; everyone at the Litquake Literary Festival, the San Francisco Writer's Grotto, and in the Bay Area literary community at large, who make our city the best place in the world to be a book lover; all our friends and supporters online, from Central Booking to South by Southwest to Readerville, who recognize that the future is now and want to be a part of it; Rhodes Fishburne, Nan Talese, Pamela Ribon, Oscar Vilallon, Roman Mars, Nicole Sawaya, Nicolson Baker, Kevin Ferguson, Wendy Sheanin, Tamara Strauss, Sean McDonald, Teresa LeYung Ryan, Edward Nawotka, Lissa Warren, and MJ Rose, who were there from the beginning; my friends and family who said I could do it; and Suzan Foley, who knew all along.

To continue the conversation, join us at www.bookmark now.net and www.kevinsmokler.com.

Kevin

CONTRIBUTOR BIOS

Christian Bauman is author of the novels *The Ice Beneath You* (Scribner, 2002) and *Voodoo Lounge* (Touchstone, 2005) and a regular contributor to NPR's *All Things Considered*. Born in Easton, Pennsylvania, in June 1970, Bauman grew up in Hunterdon County, New Jersey, and lived a year in India when he was thirteen. He joined the army at age twenty-one and served tours of duty in Somalia and Haiti. Honorably discharged in 1995, he spent the next four years traveling and performing on the North American folk music circuit. Currently an editor-at-large for the literary magazine *Identity Theory.com*, Christian Bauman lives with his wife and daughters in Bucks County, Pennsylvania.

Tom Bissell is the author of a travel narrative, *Chasing the Sea*, and a short story collection, *God Lives in St. Petersburg*; he is also the coauthor of a humor book, *Speak, Commentary*. He writes often for *Harper's* and *The Believer*, lives (most of the time) in New York City, and is really looking forward to playing Grand Theft Auto IV: San Andreas.

Nico Cary was born and raised in Berkeley, California, and is currently a sophomore at the University of California at Berkeley. He credits "most if not all" of his development as a writer to Youth Speaks and hopes to one day be a teacher.

Tracy Chevalier grew up in Washington, D.C. After graduating from Oberlin College, she moved to London, where she still lives with her husband and son. She worked for a few years as a reference book editor before leaving office life to do an M.A. in creative writing. She has written four novels, including *The Lady and the Unicorn*, *Falling Angels*, *The Virgin Blue*, and the international best seller *Girl with a Pearl Earring*.

Paul Collins edits the Collins Library imprint of McSweeney's Books, and his work has appeared in *New Scientist* and the *Village Voice*. The author most recently of *Sixpence House: Lost in a Town of Books* and *Not Even Wrong: Adventures in Autism*, Collins currently lives in Iowa City.

Meghan Daum is the author of the best-selling essay collection *My Misspent Youth* and the critically acclaimed novel *The Quality of Life Report*, which was a *New York Times* Notable Book in 2003. Her articles and essays have appeared in the *New Yorker*, *Harper's*, *GQ*, *Vogue*, *New York*, the *Los Angeles Times*, and the *New York Times Book Review*. She lives in Los Angeles. More information can be found at www.meghandaum.com.

Kelley Eskridge is the author of the *New York Times* Notable Book *Solitaire*, as well as internationally published short fiction and essays. Her work has won the Astraea Prize and has been shortlisted for the Nebula, Tiptree, Endeavour, and Spectrum Awards, as well as adapted for television. She's a staff writer for @U2 (www.atu2.com). She lives in Seattle with Nicola Griffith and is working on a new novel. Join her for a virtual pint at www.kelleyeskridge.com.

Paul Flores is the author of the Josephine Miles Award–winning novel *Along the Border Lies* (Creative Arts Books, 2001). He has been performing spoken word for national audiences since 1996 and has been featured at numerous national spoken word venues including *Russell Simmons Presents: Def Poetry* on HBO. He is the program director of Youth Speaks, the nation's largest presenter of spoken word for teenagers. He lives in Oakland, California.

Nell Freudenberger has taught English in Bangkok and New Delhi. Her first book, *Lucky Girls,* won the Pen/Faulkner Malamud Award for short fiction. She lives in New York City.

Glen David Gold is the author of a novel, *Carter Beats the Devil*, and has published work in *McSweeneys, Playboy,* the *New York Times Sunday Magazine*, and many, many places no one has ever heard of. He has done other cool stuff, too, but if you've looked him up on Google, you know that already.

Stephanie Elizondo Griest is the author of *Around the Bloc: My Life in Moscow, Beijing, and Havana* (Villard/Random House, 2004) and has written for the *New York Times*, the *Washington Post*, the Associated Press, and *Latina* magazine. She once drove forty-five thousand miles across the United States as a correspondent for *The Odyssey*, a history Web site for kids, and she currently directs an anticensorship youth activist organization. She performs and teaches creative writing nationwide. Visit her Web site at www.aroundthebloc.com.

Nicola Griffith (www.nicolagriffith.com) is the author of four novels and coeditor of the *Bending the Landscape* series. Her essays, stories, and books have been translated into several languages and have won a variety of awards. She lives and plays in Seattle.

Howard Hunt is the author of *Young Men on Fire*. He lives in Prague, where he is currently at work on a collection of short stories.

Adam Johnson teaches creative writing at Stanford University. He is the author of *Emporium*, a collection of short stories, and *Parasites like Us*, a novel. His work has appeared in *Harper's, Esquire,* and the *Paris Review*.

Dan Kennedy is the author of *Loser Goes First* (Random House/
Crown, 2003). His work can also be found in *Created in Darkness by
Troubled Americans: The Best of McSweeney's, Humor Category*
(Knopf, 2004). He lives in New York City and commutes to Los An-
geles occasionally to take very vague meetings about working on
something that someone else has already started or changed. See
how vague? Anyway, these meetings are usually in a Japanese
Restaurant near Wilshire Boulevard.

Robert Lanham is the author of the beach-towel classic The Emer-
ald Beach Trilogy (*Pre-Coitus, Coitus,* and *Aftermath*). More recent
works include *Food Court Druids, Cherohonkees and Other Creatures
Unique to the Republic,* and *The Hipster Handbook.* Lanham's writing
has appeared in the *New York Times, Playboy,* and *Time Out.* He is
the editor and founder of www.freewilliamsburg.com and works at
Foot Locker on the weekends. Lanham lives in Brooklyn, New York,
with a Wiccan ferret.

Vivien Mejia is a writer living and working in Los Angeles. She is a
contributing editor to *Latina* magazine and has written for the *Drew
Carey Show* and *Just Shoot Me.* She is currently working on both a
novel and a screenplay.

Benjamin Nugent grew up in Cambridge and Amherst, Massachusetts, and graduated from Reed College with a B.A. in English literature. Nugent is the author of the biography *Elliott Smith and the Big
Nothing* (DaCapo, 2004), and he has written for *Time, New York,* and
the *New York Times Book Review.* He lives in Brooklyn, New York.

Neal Pollack is the semi-well-known author of *The Neal Pollack
Anthology of American Literature, Never Mind the Pollacks,* and *Alter-
nadad.* He writes for *Vanity Fair, Salon, Nerve, The Stranger,* and many
other publications. By the time you read this, he may have sold a TV
pilot or had a screenplay optioned. He lives in Austin, Texas, and occasionally Los Angeles, with his family.

Pamela Ribon is a screenwriter and the author of *Why Girls Are Weird* (Downtown Press, 2003), a novel based on her own experiences with her hugely successful Web site Pamie.com. Her work can also be seen at TelevisionWithoutPity.com, where she writes snarky recaps of today's most self-important television shows. Pamela lives in Los Angeles with her husband, Stephen Falk, who is her favorite writer. Her second novel will be published in 2006.

Michelle Richmond is the author of the novel *Dream of the Blue Room* and the story collection *The Girl in the Fall-Away Dress*, which received the Associated Writing Progress Award for Short Fiction. Her stories and essays have appeared in *Glimmer Train*, *Other Voices*, *Salon*, the *San Francisco Chronicle*, and elsewhere. She teaches writing in San Francisco and edits the online literary journal *Fiction Attic*.

Douglas Rushkoff is the author of 10 best-selling books on new media and popular culture, including *Cyberia*, *Media Virus*, *Playing the Future*, and *Nothing Sacred: The Truth About Judaism*, *Coercion*, winner of the Marshall Mcluhan Award for best media book. Rushkoff also wrote the acclaimed novels *Ecstasy Club* and *Exit Strategy*, the graphic novel, *Club Zero-G*, and wrote and hosted the award-winning documentaries "The Merchants of Cool" and "The Persuaders" for PBS's *Frontline*. His commentaries air on CBS's *Sunday Morning* and NPR's *All Things Considered*, and have appeared in publications such as *The New York Times* and *Time*. The founder of the Narrative Lab at NYU's Interactive Telecommunications Program, Douglas Rushkoff lectures at conferences and universities around the world on media, art, society, and change. He lives in Brooklyn, New York, with his wife and daughter.

Tara Bray Smith lives and works in Brooklyn, New York. She is the author of *West of Then: A Mother, a Daughter, and a Journey Past Paradise*.

K. M. Soehnlein is the author of the novels *The World of Normal Boys*, which won the Lambda Literary Award for best gay fiction, and

You Can Say You Knew Me When, from Kensington Books (Fall 2005). He lives in San Francisco, where he teaches creative writing, works as a freelance copywriter and editor, and is part of the art and music collective The Cubby.

Elizabeth Spiers is the editor-in-chief of mediabistro.com. She was previously a contributing writer and editor at *New York Magazine* and the founding editor of Gawker.com. She has also written for the *New York Times,* the *New York Post, Salon, Radar, Black Book,* and *The Face.* A native of Alabama, she lives in New York City.

RESOURCES

NOTE: I have used all of these resources at one time or another. Some I use every day. But since I am not made of titanium, this is a suggestive and incomplete list. If I have not included your favorite blog, book, magazine or Web site, it is not personal. Pinky swear.

Web Sites of Authors in This Book Who Have Them

Christian Bauman
www.christianbauman.com/

Tracy Chevalier
www.tchevalier.com

Meghan Daum
www.meghandaum.com

Kelley Eskridge
www.kelleyeskridge.com

Stephanie Elizondo Griest
www.aroundthebloc.com

Nicola Griffith
www.nicolagriffith.com

Dan Kennedy
reallysmalltalk.com/

Robert Lanham
  www.foodcourtdruids.com
Neal Pollack
  www.nealpollack.com
Pamela Ribon
  www.pamie.com
Michelle Richmond
  www.michellerichmond.com
Douglas Rushkoff
  www.rushkoff.com
Tara Bray Smith
  www.tarabraysmith.com
Karl Soehnlein
  www.normalboys.com/

Reading at Risk Report (June 2004)
  www.nea.gov/news/pub/ReadingAtRisk.pdf

Blogs I Read Every Day (or Just About)

Beatrice.com (www.beatrice.com)
  Long-running blog/e-zine by New York–based book critic Ron Hogan. Includes an extensive collection of interviews with contemporary authors.

Bookslut.com (bookslut.com/blog)
  Immensely popular Chicago-based blog of daily book and publishing news. Founded and edited by Jessa Crispin.

Backstory (http://mjroseblog.typepad.com/backstory/)
  Author M. J. Rose features a weekly essay from an author discussing the origins of her or his most recent novel.

Buzz, Balls, Hype (http://mjroseblog.typepad.com/buzz_balls_hype/)
  Another M. J. Rose project on contemporary book marketing and publicity issues.

Confessions of an Idiosyncratic Mind (www.sarahweinman.com/)
Focuses on mystery novels and thrillers. Edited by Sarah Weinman, mystery critic for the *Baltimore Sun*.

Cupcake Series Blog (http://cupcakeseries.blogspot.com/)
Supports the NYC Cupcake Reading series, featuring the city's best women writers. Discusses gender issues in publishing, favorite female authors, and "the evils of chick lit."

The Elegant Variation (www.elegant.com)
Daily publishing news, author interviews, and book reviews from L.A.-based screenwriter Mark Sarvas.

Librarian.net (www.librarian.net)
All things libraries, librarians, and the freedom to read without the government spying on your choices. Run by Vermont-based librarian Jessamyn West.

Maud Newton (www.maudnewton.com/blog/)
The book blog all the others read. Maud is a Brooklyn-based attorney who also edits and writes fiction.

Moby Lives (www.mobylives.com/)
One of the original book Web logs, fiercely and thoroughly edited by Dennis Loy Johnson, founder of the Melville House Press.

My Favorite Book-Related Magazines
(Print)

The Believer
www.believermag.com
Very long interviews with authors as well as essays about books and bibliophilic whatnots.

Black Issues Book Review
www.bibookreview.com/
Bimonthly discussion of books by and about African-Americans.

Bookmarks Magazine
www.bookmarksmagazine.com/
A monthly compendium of book reviews from multiple sources.

Rain Taxi

www.raintaxi.com/

A powerhouse quarterly out of Minneapolis. Also produces a reading series and a line of chapbooks.

Three Penny Review

www.threepennyreview.com/

Supa-heady lit journal out of Berkeley, California. These people have read more than you ever will.

Women's Review of Books

www.wellesley.edu/WomensReview/

A feminist stronghold for over twenty years. Based at Wellesley College.

(Online)

Arts & Letters Daily

www.aldaily.com

A massive online broadsheet of hundreds of links to new books, arts and culture news, and political commentary. Updated six days a week and just as dizzying as it sounds. Owned by the *Chronicle of Higher Education*.

Arts Journal

www.artsjournal.com

A "Daily Digest of Arts, Culture and Ideas" edited by Seattle-based journalist Douglas McLennan. Includes sections on publishing, media, and dance as well as blogs by renowned critics and several newsletters. You could get lost here for weeks.

The Backlist

www.thebacklist.net

Superb e-zine focusing on contemporary African-American publishing and literary issues. Published by Emerson College graduate student Felicia Pride.

Good Reports

http://www.goodreports.net

Essays and critiques by Canadian bibliophile Alex Good.

Identity Theory

www.identitytheory.com/

"A literary website, sort of." Hundreds of interviews, reviews and essays. Founded and edited by Matt Borondy of Gainsville, Florida, with help from about a dozen other terrifyingly smart people.

McSweeney's Internet Tendency

www.mcsweeneys.net/

The online companion to the revolutionary publisher. I'm not exactly sure which came first, but the Web site is updated just about every day.

New Pages

www.newpages.com

A gianormous portal of links and news focusing on nonmainstream books, magazines, literary journals, independent bookstores, and record labels. Published out of Alpena, Michigan, by Casey and Denise Hill, who are either related, married, or a happy coincidence.

Small Publishers I Support and/or Who Have Sent Me Free Stuff

AK Press

www.akpress.com/

Oakland, California–based workers' co-op which publishes and distributes radical materials.

Drawn & Quarterly

www.drawnandquarterly.com/

Montreal-based comics and graphic-novel powerhouse. Publishes Adrian Tomine, Julie Doucet, Debbie Dreschler, and Seth.

Fantagraphics

www.fantagraphics.com

Seattle-based champion of the graphic novel. Publishes R. Crumb, Chris Ware, Dan Clows, Jessica Abel and handles reprints of *Peanuts*.

Manic D. Press

www.manicdpress.com
 San Francisco house specializing in poetry, performance writings, and literary fiction with an urban edge.

Seal Press

www.sealpress.com/
 Seattle-based, mostly nonfiction press, focusing on women's issues and authors. Famous for anthologies.

Seven Stories Press

www.sevenstories.com/
 Fiction and writings of conscience. Has published Ralph Nader, Howard Zinn, Kurt Vonnegut, and Angela Davis.

So New Media

www.sonewmedia.com
 Ultra-mirco publisher out of Austin, Texas, that made its name publishing books for popular Web loggers. Uses a laser printer and the U.S. Mail.

Soft Skull Press

www.softskull.com/
 New York outfit specializing in cultural criticism and poetry. Edgy and smart.

Conferences and Festivals Worth Crashing

The 215 Festival (Philadelphia, PA)

www.215festival.com/
 Annual confluence of literature, righteous music, and arts-inspired lunacy. As hip as these things get.

AWP Annual Conference (rotating locations)

www.awpwriter.org/conference/index.htm
 AWP stands for Associated Writing Programs, so we're mostly talking about students, professors, and administrators. Stuffier than the average book-related affair but seems to be loosening up. A great event if your goal is teaching writing or studying it in an academic setting.

Book Expo America (rotating locations)

www.bookexpoamerica.com

The annual Mardi Gras of the book business, except that it happens in early June. Thousands of booksellers, publishers, authors, and journalists convene every year to mingle and report on the state of this nutty business. Also, famously media-friendly, so I'd recommend asking your local college newspaper/radio station/Web zine to fax in a press pass request for you. Oh, and the parties are legendary.

Book Punk (Austin, TX)

www.bookpunk.com/

"Literature, Rock n' Roll, Beer" usually on the same raucous stage. Normally a monthly happening.

Idea Festival (Lexington, KY)

www.ideafestival.com

New annual conference on the scene with an old-school premise: Throw a bunch of really smart, creative people in the same room, get them talking, and see what happens. Had a bunch of poets and performers in 2004. Who knows where it will go next?

Info Demo (Atlanta, GA)

www.jsassociate.com/bpa.htm

Half variety show, half lecture series, all art. Sporadic but always worth it.

L.A. Times Festival of Books (Los Angeles, CA)

www.latimes.com/extras/festivalofbooks/

The biggest of its kind on the West Coast and dripping with star power thanks to its Hollywood locale. Some of the educational sessions attract thousands of attendees. Annually in April or May.

Litquake (San Francisco, CA)

www.litquake.org/

The Bay Area's biggest, baddest literary festival. Nearly two hundred authors (including Dave Eggers, Amy Tan, and Lemony Snicket) were featured in the nine-day 2004 festival. Includes readings, panels, film screenings, and a literary-themed pub crawl. Usually in October.

Little Gray Books Lecture Series (Brooklyn, NY)

www.littlegraybooks.com

A near-monthly how-to series of talks featuring writers artists, actors, radio producers, and musicians. Hosted by former-agent-turned-arts-impresario John Hodgeman.

New York Is Book Country (NYC)

www.nyisbookcountry.com/

Annual celebration of books, authors, and reading. Held in the fall.

Nieman Conference on Narrative Journalism (Cambridge, MA)

www.nieman.harvard.edu

Annual winter gathering of the smartest journalists in the land. Past speakers have included Ken Burns, Hilton Als, Adrian Nicole LeBlanc, and Susan Orlean.

South by Southwest (Austin, TX)

www.sxsw.com

Annual March gathering of creative professionals in music, film, and the Web, with an increasing author presence. Although attended by plenty of suits, the focus remains on creativity and innovation, not product launches and quarterly reports. Still affordable enough for interested amateurs and hence draws a bunch.

Texas Book Festival (Austin, TX)

www.texasbookfestival.org

Annual fall festival benefiting libraries throughout the Lone Star State. Normally draws a prestigious cadre of authors and a dedicated corps of volunteers.

Virginia Festival of the Book (Charlottesville, VA)

www.vabook.org

One of the strongest of the smaller regional festivals with an exceedingly friendly class of attendees. Annually in the spring.

Start Here

Booksense

www.booksense.com

The easiest way to find and support your local independent bookstore.

Poets & Writers

www.pw.org

An aspiring writer's best friend. The most comprehensive and honest publication on how to work and live as a writer.

Publisher's Lunch

www.caderbooks.com

A subscription-only daily briefing of the publishing industry.

PW Daily

www.publishersweekly.com

Free e-mail edition of *Publishers Weekly*, the trade journal of the book biz.

Readerville

www.readerville.com

Vibrant online community of bibliophiles and writers and a daily reminder that there are more of us out there than we think.